What Your

Eyes Cain't

See...

The Anthology

edited by

Yaminah Ahmad & Kim Caldwell

Goode Stuff Publishing
·
Atlanta GA

Goode Stuff Publishing

Copyright © 2004 Goode Stuff Publishing

Published in the USA by
Goode Stuff Publishing
Atlanta, GA
www.goodestuffentertainment.com

ISBN: 0-9712095-0-2
Editors: Yaminah Ahmad & Kim Caldwell
Layout & Cover Design: Rod Hollimon
Cover Artwork: Alan Grimes

Acknowledgements

The Goode Stuff family would like to thank Jihad and Janette Ahmad with true sincerity for having the foresight to believe in our vision.

INTRODUCTION

During the tender years of youth, dreams are often crafted and constructed. Very few survive, many are simply refurbished and supposedly "upgraded" by the cynicism of an illusionary reality. I— have always wanted to write and perform and create. I can remember the first book that I ever digested as well as the first time my voice echoed through the ears of a captive audience. The latter being no more of an adrenaline rush than the first. Both experiences made me feel strong and alive.

Maybe if my spirit would have been one that could conform to the parameters of this world, the rules and regulations of a grafted concept of accomplishment and defeat, I would have popped my pencil and silenced my voice a long time ago. I could not. Now, a couple of decades from the initial thought of one of the few decisions that I have passionately stood by in 29 years, I am proud to present the newest member of history: Goode Stuff Publishing.

As a company, Goode Stuff has taken on the role of cultural curators. We have vowed to take on projects that document the full scope of our generation, instead of, allowing our legacy to fall to the perils of Viacom.

It would be sacrilegious for me to not acknowledge the power of the hip-hop influence over every aspect of Generation X's movements. From the corporate offices to the pages of contemporary literature, we are wrapped in the love of rap. This is something to be proud of... what is not a crown of achievement is that the same spirits, who should be rooted in the soils of "Fight The Power", have allowed those powers to dictate the integrity of their existence. The dexterity of what they will ultimately be remembered for...

The first step in the battle to define who we are now and what we will become in the very near future is the ability to control what brush paints our portrait. GoodeStuff Publishing is the resurgence of such spirits as James Baldwin and Fred Hampton. We are the new bearers of the torch. Those that refuse to accept that their voice is prerecorded in oval offices or written into the bylaws of a system that thrives on their very inability to recognize not only the power of the legacy before them, but the legacy that they are responsible for creating in the present tense.

As the publisher of such a close knit network of poets, writers, visual artist, and revolutionaries it has been far beyond a privilege to put together Goode Stuff Publishing's first anthology. The title, <u>What Your Eyes Cain't See</u>, speaks volumes to the David can defeat Goliath spirit that is embodied by the individuals that have contributed their souls to this project.

The concept for this anthology was born from a conversation between Jon Goode and Amir Sulaiman that I was later included in. It was early fall 2003 and an adequate portion of the upper east coast had just suffered a massive power outage. Because of the state of the nation at that time, a state that has since elevated ten fold, most people contemplated the fear of further terrorist attacks. My comrades, on the other hand, wasted no mind space with the minimal thoughts of bombs and Al-Qaida (especially when we live in the very country that trains and supports such creations); rather, they pondered the inevitable fate of this world that will one day have to deal with the reflection in the mirror, void of the technological crutches that nurture our daily disillusions.

What happens when the lights go out? And the TV doesn't work. And Viacom lacks the ability to spit the soundtrack of your life through the FM airwaves? What happens when you have to find light in the midst of darkness? I speak of this search in a more tangible perspective because on a mental and spiritual level this scavenger hunt is present in our everyday lives.

Once the concept for a collection of fiction, based upon the idea of seeing truth beyond the surface, developed a heartbeat it was the responsibility of Goode Stuff Publishing to ensure that it was fed the proper nutrients for a viable existence. We had to choose the correct writers. The selection process was actually without hardship. The writers were chosen for, not only, their literary abilities, but their desire to achieve what has been labeled as impossible - to raise the bar in the achievements of those with the blessing of melanin.

The stories contained within this anthology are great works that force the mind's eye to delve beyond the superficial. They will require the reader to look within for open and honest answers that will challenge what has been forced on us as the normal train of thought. Our prayers are that as Goode Stuff Publishing embarks on this less traveled trail of true empowerment the reader will choose to travel also. As we grow, so will the strength of our generation and generations to follow; those who will be responsible for picking up wherever The Most High blesses us to leave off.

Malik Salaam
Publisher

Table of Contents

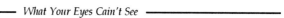

What a family talks about in the evening, the child will talk about in the morning.

—Kenya Proverb

Runnin' The Block

Malik Salaam

Baltimore, Maryland. The Ravens. The… whatever. Don't know and really don't give a fuck… Just really not my kind of city. I remember surveying the barren land for the first time. Blue skies were charcoaled gray by shipyards and industrial smoke… I'm talkin' a thick haze. For miles, I was absorbed by blocks and blocks of concrete. Surrounded by despair. Heroine addicts scratching and................ nodding on the stoops of abandoned row houses. Zombies roamed the streets in broad daylight. I mean, I've stayed right up on Simpson and Sunset in some sheet rock apartments watching dykes shoot out at odd hours of the night; but them Baltimore Blocks – now that shit is a little ridiculous.

At any rate, my manager (which is really me with a suit, tie, and my most polished grammatical skills) booked myself for a performance showcase in The Great Land of Depression. And against my better judgment, I called a couple of my comrades. We jumped in The Happy Van (which is a lot doper than The Mystery Machine) and shot up I-85 to the I-95 connector. The road, for me, is always a way to gain some sort of perspective on what is going on in my life. I really can't pinpoint it exactly; but somewhere in between the conversation and the carsickness, I always seem to return from my road trips with a renewed faith in my ability to master this game called life.

It was almost the sunset's grand finale when JG, Sulaiman and I eased on up the bridge, which leads right into B-More. The usually drab city was somehow held in some all-powerful divergence. The charcoal encrusted atmosphere was replaced with a bright mix of burgundy and fuchsia with streaks of gold, glowing and bouncing off the side of the metropolis' skyline. Lights from office buildings danced against the backdrop of creation. The scenery was captivating. And the Happy Van, usually alive with mind-blowing conversation, philosophical epiphanies, and satirical tall tales, fell into a state of meditation.

"Man, what the hell is that in the middle of the road," JG inquired, breaking the silence, and speaking more to himself than to anyone in particular. "Is that a … dog?"

For some reason, I immediately broke out of my trance. And there in the distance was a small creature running fast along the length of the bridge. I glanced quickly into the side mirror, snapped my head to slightly gaze out of the back windows, and darted my eyes back to the pup. *Where had he come from?* Amazingly, there were no cars in front of him. It was almost as if he appeared from nowhere. But behind The Happy Van, the traffic was thickening. As we approached the small tan and white beast, my heart began to ache and my eyes instantly glazed over. This moafucka was pumping with everything he had. His eyes peeled wide, occasionally glancing behind him, but primarily, concentrating on the now with no real hope for the future. His tongue was hanging out – aware of the fact that his life was on the line.

"Damn...."

But there was nothing we could do for him. For some strange reason, I remembered Mario.

*   *   *

I met Mario at the very beginning of my adolescent years. I was 14 and he was about 11 or 12 years-old. We were both working for The Brother (an ex-hoodlum turned Muslim turned businessman) selling bootleg cassette tapes and movies on VHS (I'm talkin' *Coming to America* when it was still in the theaters) on the busiest corners in the Atlanta Metropolitan area.

The gig was my first unsupervised experience with the streets. Before then, I'd always been under the watchful eye of cats much older than myself, cats that did a pretty good job of keeping me out of harm's way.

"Got all the latest and greatest music. Check me out."

"Wachu got in the box lil' man?"

"Gospel, Jazz, Rhythm/Blues, and Soul... What kinda music do you like? " Never waiting for a reply. I would reach into my box, "Got that new Luther 'Here and Now'," practically shoving it into an unexpected hand. I was something of a baby hustler. Fourteen years young and I could talk the nigga choking the life right out of Abraham's ass to loosen his grip. I was good, but that nigga, Mario... now that was an absolute talent. Some days he would come in and work half a day, and top the sales of everybody in our crew. The thing that amazed me most about Mario was that he didn't even have a sales pitch.

"Got them tapes. Check me out." His voice and mannerism, evidently, had some sort of authoritative magnetism that would draw the consumer to him. Then, as soon as he had them within arms reach, his hands would start reaching in and out of the box with such speed and precision. If my memory serves me correctly, which sometimes it does and sometimes it doesn't, *"Fist of Fury"* was the first time Bruce Lee introduced that type of human speed to the world. I mean, this moafucka would sell out every single tape he had in his carrying case (which was usually nothing more than a stolen plastic milk crate) on several occasions.

You see, to do this was an exceptional task, even for the most skilled salesman. Let the truth be told: with the beauty of my budding mouthpiece, I had only achieved this feat once. To say the least, Mario amazed me. In retrospect, I think that it is only natural for individuals to walk into new situations and find an object, whether tangible or not, that holds them in a temporary state of captivity. For my generation, it was usually a destructive fixation. What I think was done, systematically, was find counterrevolutionary material that attracted our God-given souljah-like spirits, and to use those materials to foster the environment so the government no longer had to actively participate in our demise, unless, it was for their personal joy and satisfaction. And so the impoverished Black communities became acquainted with: *the dope boy in the trap.*

Now, Mario lived in the back of East Lake Meadows. It was '89 and crack had just hit Amerikkka hard as hell. I think, maybe, just two years prior, I remember browsing through a publication called, "The Weekly Reader," which I received ever, so often in grade school. I stumbled across an article about this really cheap drug that was mixed with cocaine, baking soda, and a chemical that had some sort of technical name (Later on, I simply knew this chemical as "comeback"). But now, the entire country was in an uproar. Amerikkka was plagued with the Reagan/Bush Era, which, at that particular time, was the Bush And Whoever-The-Fuck-Else Era. Young Black men were becoming millionaires, going to jail, and dying in the same gust of wind. And "The Meadows" which had earned the nickname, *Lil' Vietnam,* was like most housing projects: totally infested with this narcotic phenomenon.

I always new that Mario did more than sold bootleg tapes. He had the whole drug dealer starter kit: two different colors of the first Michael Jordan's, a beeper, two gold fronts (from the dentist office downtown where the 107 bus let you off), and a different pair of Paco and Used denims for every day of the week. Even with Mario's high sells margin, it was highly unlikely that this type of fabulous life was possible sellin' "Piece of My Love" by Guy. But like most seasoned drug dealers, Mario's life outside of the bootleg racket was vague to say the least. So when Mario told me to come through Saturday and kick it with him and his kinfolk, I was completely ecstatic.

After carefully listening to Mario's instructions: "Walk down Second Ave., right after Austin, you will see a trail on your left. Just cut through the woods and you'll see me." I planned out every detail of the coming Sabbath day. It began with my initial plan to evade work and my mother in one clean swoop, and the exact particulars of what gear I would rock for this auspicious occasion. Now being somewhat fresh off the porch, I had not yet grasped the concept that fear and caution were two very separate, but necessary beasts.

The times that I was being reared in... speaking of course about the climate of the society (as opposed to my direct community life) mandated a set of unwritten laws... Laws that were rapped about in our music and personified by the gatekeepers of our culture. We didn't fear shit and the ignorance of youth threw caution to the wind. So, I (being the *N.W.A* that I was) decided that my experience would be far more adventurous if I took the quickest route, which was straight through the rice fields of *Lil' Vietnam*.

        *   *   *

"I know these little pretty moafuckas ain't walking down my fuckin' street!"

For bragging rights, I dragged one of my homeboys from the all-black, all-Muslim private school I attended to embark on this monumental adventure with me. Now *this guy* (I will just call him *This Guy* and pretty much leave it at that) convinced me that his street credibility was impeccable. It was not. The first leg of our journey was easy – no glitches in the Matrix. No troubles on the horizon. Given, this ease we were experiencing could have been the direct effect of the long abandoned red clay field; it ushered us into the projects long before we entered the first set of buildings. Regardless, our minds were telling us that we were ghetto and our walks became strides and our chest began to widen.... We were roosters.

That is until our (or maybe it was just *This Guy's*) presence was detected. The reality was for me that even though the outside of my home did not reflect the beautiful décor of the housing projects, the inner workings of my single-parent, split level home had all the fixings that ghetto life provided. Food stamps. No lights. And a mother whose bitterness was only heightened with the constant reminder of my father's existence through his reflection in my eyes.

"I know these niggas ain't... What tha fuck?"

The only option was to run. And I ain't talking about a slow trot or a ginger jog – I'm speaking of the 40 in 4 seconds flat. I'm talking balls out from the last utterance of "what tha fuck" until we arrived on safe, dry land... Mario's block. I can only remember a few times in my life where the presence of another man made my heart skip a beat and brought tears of joy to my eyes. Despite Mario's uncontrollable laughter, this is what Mario's presence evoked in me... relief.

"Nigga," his words lost somewhere in his chuckle, "I thought I told you to walk down Second Avenue. Shit, y'all niggas fuckin wit' Carl Lewis."

I just shook my head, wondering if we were even being chased, and if so, where the hell did the hunter disappear?

"C'mon, shawdy. We up here on the hill."

The hill seemed like it was its own planet, some great big infrastructure that sat in its own orbit. *The hill...* metaphysically speaking, was bigger than the projects themselves. It was behind the last row of buildings with a clear view of the adjoining parking lot, and with Mario's binoculars, which was draped around his neck, you could see the only entrance into The Meadows. To our backs were some woods and a trail. A trap... absolutely... NO WAY OUT.

It was about two other niggas on *the hill*: one cat who never made any formal introduction. I guess it was because his jaw was made of the same stone as that of the rest of his face. Then, there was this other cat... Sam. The court jester equipped with the tattered clothing and a bomb of crack that he called his happy sack. Hanging from one of the trees was a large rag, which was lit and smothered every five minutes. It produced enough smoke for The War on Southern Mosquitoes, which infected the entire area. Outside of that, there were several empty cans of Ole English, a couple of lighters without lighter fluid, and what appeared to be a dirty pamper, which was actually a stash spot for excess dope. And then, there was Mario.

An 11... or 12 year-old with a fresh new pair of Jordan's, a dingy white t-shirt and a bank roll of money that he seemed to count at his leisure, without any fear (of course, this was right before dope-boys were getting their heads blown off for 10 dollars). He had an arm full of mosquito bites, and a watchful eye on every shady individual that made their way through the smoked trail. But a couple of things struck me as peculiar.

First, there was the constant trail of visitors – all with different shapes, sizes and genders. All walking so swiftly through the woods that they barely even touched the ground long enough to snap a twig. Every once in a while a few distinguished individuals would pull into the parking lot... pushin' every make and model car you could imagine. Although there was an array of people being served, each of them held an extremely distinctive look in their eyes.

It was a distant look. A look that yearned for something that was so far out of their grasp that their eyes were glazed with sadness and grief. A grief that was multiplied several times over because, whatever it was they were attempting to capture, this thing that was so unattainable, it had them bound to the chase. Forever indebted to *this thing* that would never, could never, promise a return. They were addicted.

The other factor in this equation I found completely outlandish was the fact that Mario was 11... or 12 and these other two cats were, maybe, 11... or 12 years older than him. But it was clear that Mario was in charge – in charge, but not respected. It was as if a force that lacked a physical presence, but yet, implemented a chain of command, orchestrated fear from a far off land. There was a feeling of intensity, which reeked of betrayal, danger... and loyalty that barely scratched the surface.

Despite all of this, as the day flew by, I found somewhat of a comfort around these lost souls. There was always a beer to drink or a joint to smoke or a needy customer who quickly became the butt of Sam's cruel and hilarious jokes. Jokes that were more for his amusement than anybody else's. At one point, a regular name Cocamo took *Mr. Stoneface* to the side of the building to suck him dry in exchange for a bag of shake (shake being what is left over from the bulk of the product.... the shit that could barely be sold).

"'Ey, shawdy, let's walk down to my house real quick," Mario blurted out as he peered through the binoculars. He looked at his two employees. They nodded their heads, held their positions, and me, Mario, and *this guy* started down *the hill*. Mario's walk was quick. About halfway through the parking lot Mario was stopped. A woman whispered something in his ear. He shook his head; his eyes shuddered with anger and compassion. And he reached into his pocket and hesitantly placed a bag in the woman's hand. Without any acknowledgement, she began to scurry through an opening in the buildings.

"Ma," Mario screamed.

I looked around trying to get a visual on who he was talking to.

"Momma, I know you hear me."

The woman turned around.

Mario's eyes shuddered with anger and compassion. "I don't want to see you up on that fuckin hill."

*   *   *

As we approached the small tan and white beast, my heart began to ache and my eyes instantly glazed over. This moafucka was pumping with everything he had. His eyes peeled wide, occasionally glancing behind him, but primarily, concentrating on the now with no real hope for the future. His tongue was hanging out... aware of the fact that his life was on the line.

"Damn..."

Shoplifting is A Violation
by Malik Salaam

What happens —
when the times change
and pain is everyday routine.
They closed down Techwood and The Cap
'cause housing projects/slap the taste
clean outta some NRA/KKK card carrying members' mouth
somehow, destroys the city's scenery.
South of the Mason Dixie line... a sign of the times
my childhood completely missed me.
You know my history:
my father was absent and now the present danger
is parents and kids are strangers
because he
is a man-child in the promise land
and she
is a broken hearted chick
impregnated by some half man
full punk
a welfare mom and her son

got one in the chamber and
a back-up pump in the trunk

cause an adolescents youth ain't about being young no mo'

its 44s and calicos
peach/white owls and
barely midgrade marijuana sold as '*dro*
kids ain't simply playing cops and robbers
they are actually hitting licks for their next meal
put a few in your skull
mash out and peel
socially ill
because my youth has been stolen,
and wrapped in raps about
how fly it is to trap and
we buy into the lies and crap
even though deep down we know
that it is

a big: whateva

when hollow tips spit from the open end
of a Beretta
and a twelve year old lays
shakin' and convulsing
his justification is:

pa'tna I'm chasin that chedda'.

Kinfolk,
Like Pac I'm prayin' for betta days
where kids play...
and don't have to worry about
gunpowder stealin' their youth

The Rubicon

Jon Goode

It had been a long time coming and by a long time, I mean all summer long. Hank Junior has finally crossed the Rubicon. You may wonder what sparks this Rubicon reference. Mr. Calahan taught us in history class earlier today that The Rubicon is the river Caesar crossed to declare war on Pompey. Well, Hank ain't exactly Caesar and I ain't exactly Pompey, but war has definitely been declared. Plus, they say the best way to memorize a word is to use it in everyday conversation and, thusly, RUBICON.

You may wonder what exactly has Hank done to have such a usually reserved, peace loving kid like myself so upset and recklessly using world history vocabulary words. Well, I won't belabor the point, I'll come straight to it. Hank uttered the street battle cry, the universal call to arms, the two word phrase that ensures that a donnybrook must ensue…Your Mama!

Oh, and with such venom he spoke the words. They rather dripped from his lips more than they were spoken. All the girls laughed and the boys began to encourage a brawl with little quips like, "I know you ain't gonna let him talk about your mama." Another interjected, "If I was you, I'd punch him in his face for talking about my mama like that," and so on and so on. The words "Your Mama" in and of themselves need no supporting motivation to insight an all out brawl, but couple them with my injured pride, my suddenly endangered reputation (although in truth, I had no reputation) and the fact that my mother had just last year passed on into the great hereafter and my path was clear. As a ten year old boy, my pride and my image in my so-called friends' eyes is everything. It's really all I have. For most pre-pubescent kids, it's all we have so, I have little choice but to get my back up, brandish my claws, bear my fangs and become cat- like on my feet as the adrenaline begins to seek out and find the reluctant warrior in me. My mother's memory and honor along with my pride and dignity have to be defended at all cost.

Now, Hank Junior is what they called big for his age. He is actually a ten year old boy just like me, but he seems to be trapped in the body of a 15 year old man. Rumor has it that his pituitary gland is overproducing like the Neptunes. His forearms seem to be the size of my thighs and the way his brow dips in the middle of his huge forehead whether he's upset or not, kind of puts you in the mind of Cro-Magnon Man or maybe a rabid Rotweiler. His breath is much more intimidating that his size. I'm not a dentist, but it seems that too many Now & Laters and not enough brushing is wreaking havoc on his teeth, which maintain a grape Now & Later tint (even if he hasn't had a piece of candy in weeks). His early jump into puberty seems to be having quite a time with his skin, which is as pock marked and craterous as the face of the moon. There is no way around it, Hank is a dental and a dermatological cash cow. He usually uses his uncommon size and haggard looks to intimidate the rest of us hygiene conscious kids with what seem to be dormant pituitaries. But I won't be intimidated today, there is too much at stake. Today he has gone too far. Today Goliath will have yet another bout with David. And this David, in the guise of yours truly, has more up his sleeve than just a sling shot and a smooth stone. This David has a cousin in the crowd ready to jump in. My cousin DeWayne (we call him Skinny) is up from Petersburg and I know that if the battle starts to go long and wrong he will join in the frey.

So here I stand, thin as a rail and trembling with anger, nerves and fear. I can feel the perspiration running down my back and the whole world seems to be moving in slow motion.

Hank looks over at me and says, "Oh, so you think I'm funny!! What you gonna do punk?"

I can't imagine why he thinks that I think that he's funny. I haven't actually said or done a thing. Then, I remember my own dental issues. It just so happens that I have one of the worst and most pronounced overbites on the planet. It always seems to give people the impression that I'm smiling or laughing at them. My fists, which I hadn't even noticed were balled, totally betray the notion of laughing smiling happiness. Hank and I approach each other as dance partners might across an empty ballroom. It's almost as if we are being magnetically drawn into this confrontation as if neither of us could pull away even if we wanted too. Our dance floor is an empty lot with patchy grass that serves as a makeshift basketball court, baseball field and horseshoe pit. News of the fight about to take place spreads like a California forest fire. There is an electric buzz that fills the air as the neighborhood kids begin to fill the lot. The guttural chants, barks and eggings on must be the same music that greeted the Roman Gladiators in the coliseum, "I who am about to die salute you!" And then, as if on que, the ritual of playground fighting begins.

We both hit our marks at center lot where we stand shoulder to shoulder. Well, rather shoulder to ribs or shoulder to biceps due to height issues, but you get the picture. We begin to circle like dirty dishwater down the drain. We begin to jostle and murmur insults and curses at one another. This part of the playground fighting ritual is performed purely to see if one gladiator can get the other to back down from pure intimidation. It's much like when two male Silver Back Orangutans are fighting over a female. One of the males will suddenly come charging out of the rainforest beating his chest and screaming as loud as he can at the other male Orangutan, just to see if he can avoid the fight and make his co-suitor run off. With Hank and me, it's just like it usually is with the Silver Backs, neither of us is going anywhere. Neither of us gave any ground. This circle we trace in the middle of the lot is our last chance for negotiation and peaceful resolution, but we can both feel the peace talks failing as the jostling turns into bumping. Then, before I know it, before I can begin to react, it happens.

Hank gives me a two handed shove to the chest. This shove if done correctly pushes the opponent off balance, sending his arms flailing about and his head and neck into a whiplash like action. Hank performs the technique flawlessly as my noggin begins to teeter tot like a bobble head doll. Were the two handed chest shove an Olympic event, Hank would have brought the gold home for the old U.S. of A that day. Olympic gold withstanding, I'm sent back about three steps as I try to regain my balance and composure. I flail my arms in an effort to regain balance and also as an exaggerated show of defiance. When my arms finally stop swinging wildly about, they come to rest in a fighting position. At the end of each arm is a trembling, small, nervous fist. Hank smiles and my overbite gives the illusion that I do to.

Hank's two handed pre-emptive strike to my chest hurt more than my feelings, and the collective gasp of "Ooooh!" from our baseball, basketball horseshoe compatriots who have suddenly turned into boxing enthusiast was the equivalent of the Arch Duke Ferdinand of Austria's assassination. And by that, I mean that in the grand scheme of things it was an insignificant event, but it signaled that there had to be a war.

Now, my father (also a thin man) had earlier in the year given me some sound advice when it comes to fighting. He looked me dead in the eye and, with as much heartfelt sincerity and concern as he could muster, with as much fatherly compassion as he could trudge from the depths of his soul he said, "Son, cheat."

He continued on by saying, "Son, you're too light to fight and you are too thin to win. So cheat! Swing first and swing often! Some people may look down on your style of fighting and call it unsportsmanlike, but as soon as they turn their backs kick their asses too. You know son, somewhere in the cosmic scheme of things, God has always had a soft spot in his heart for skinny guys and to that end, he has seen fit to bless us with the constant presence of a random brick. The divine brick of Ethiopia it is sometimes called (by who, I wondered). At sometime in life you may find yourself in a fight, in an area where there has never been construction of any sort, in the middle of the woods, 100 miles away from the nearest building and you'll look down and there it is, almost as if placed there by God himself, a brick. Let this brick be a balm to your wounds. Wield this brick well, my son!! Just as Authur had Excalibur, so too shall you have a brick." My father could be a little dramatic at times.

As all of these thoughts dance through my mind, I can hear and almost feel the presence of my father which is a rare thing seeing that he is rarely, if ever, around. Hank being smarter than he looks, but then again a stone wall is smarter than Hank looks, senses my momentary lack of concentration and launches a full scale all out attack.

For once in his and (thank God) my life, his size works against him. His pituitary has given him the body of a man, but neglected to give him the instruction manual on how to control this mountain of flesh and muscle. His first strike is way off target and awkwardly thrown. I easily duck the blow although the force behind the punch is undeniable as I can feel a rush of air as his fist moves past my head. I pop up quickly, dancing on the balls of my feet. I plant and hit him with two quick short blows to the ribs. He flinches slightly, much like a person would when unexpectedly bitten by a mosquito. He's irritated, but unharmed. My two quick counter strikes earn me "Oooooh's" from the fight hungry onlookers and I can feel my confidence rising. This must be what Cassius Clay felt like when Liston fell. The problem is, of course, being that I'm not Clay, Hank is not Liston and Hank is far from falling. I continue to dance like a gazelle and Hank continues to lumber like and elephant. His next punch is a right hook that is so choreographed it appears to almost move like the slow action sequences from The Matrix. I reward his hook with a solid punch to the stomach that bends him over at the waist and the crowd goes wild!

The playground kids are with me and my killer instinct tells me to finish Hank off. A couple of well placed blows to the chin should put an end to this contest. And once I have dispatched Goliath my baseball, basketball and horseshoe minions will no doubt take me upon their shoulders and parade me around the block to the sound of cheers and adoration. I'll, of course, be crowned the king of the lot and demand daily offerings of Sugar Daddies and Slim Jims and the sacrifice of at least one virgin Tahitian Treat per week. I'll have myself dubbed "The Hammerer of Hank" and "The Defender of The Faith." My reign shall be a long one marked with kindness to peasants and prosperity throughout the lot.

With the skill of a lion I move in for the Coupe De Grace, the final blow to send Hank to his fate and me to my glory, when suddenly the oddest thing happens. I think they call it an uppercut. I'm unsure because, to tell you the truth I didn't see it. But later, I do believe, I was told it was an uppercut. Well, whatever it was, it was definitely an up rising against my imminent monarchy. His fist, which had been mute until this point, played for me the sweetest chin music. A quiet yet aggressive tune. How could my head not dance backward for it? It must have been a great song. I was told that in honor of the tune the top of my head almost touched the middle of my back. Now, there's a song to remember.

My teeth chatter together leaving the same taste the dentist leaves after drilling a cavity, equal parts blood and enamel. My chin is Nagasaki and it has been hit with a quite nuclear strike, but it is my knees that ultimately surrender. My legs totally concede defeat and will not participate in any further destruction of my chin. And, although my chin never says it... I'm sure it's grateful. Suddenly, I see a large object coming quickly toward me, I realize that it's the ground rising up to meet me and I can only accept our inevitable embrace.

So, here I lay on my back in the lot I had until recently (although only in my mind) been dictator of. My once faithful subjects, the very peasants and peons I was going to be "oh so nice to" have instantly aligned themselves with this barbarian. I find myself, the once and future king, without a court. Oh well, I think to myself, at least the battle has come to an end. And that's when I feel it...but it can't be what I think it is. I've been gracious in defeat and I've yielded to Hanks superior uppercut...so what can this be that I keep feeling. For the life of me I don't want to believe it's true but it would seem that it is. It would appear that Hank is kicking me. Can you believe this? Kicking me! Well, I won't stand for this!! So, I lay there.

Instinctively, I time one of his kicks and grab his foot. I then use my prominent overbite to impress upon his leg my displeasure with its present course of action. The pain takes him by surprise as he bays like a wolf. I bite into his leg and hold on like a playful dog with a Frisbee until he finally joins me on the ground. Our exercise as pugilists suddenly turns Greco Roman and suddenly I remember cousin DeWayne. A feeling of relief shoots through me because I know that all I have to do is hold on and any second now DeWayne will be joining the battle. A small smile creeps across my face, but thanks to my overbite no one could tell the difference. Hank and I roll around on the ground for a while and, eventually, he tires of soiling his hands with my face and rises. He offers me one last kick as a sign that he is done. I reluctantly accept. I lay on my back staring up at the sky and think of how incredibly white the clouds are against the sky's blue backdrop.

I hear the spectators of the boxing, wrestling, biting match begin to filter out of the lot, having had their fill of my pain. I lay there for another minute or two, taking inventory of what does and does not exactly feel right on my body. The inventory ends with everything working with just a few minor pains associated with moving. I roll over and look up and the only person left in the lot is DeWayne. Obviously there was a break down in communication somewhere. He says nothing as I stand and dust myself off. He offers no words as I use my fingers to wipe the blood from the corners of my mouth. He does not break the silence as I use my shirt to wipe the blood from my nose. Then confused, confounded and curious I finally ask him,

"DeWayne?"

"Yeah?"

"Did you see the fight?"

"Yeah, I saw it."

"Did you know it was me fighting?"

"Yeah, I saw it was you"

"Well, why didn't you help me!?"

DeWayne pauses for a second and scratches his head before he answers, and what he says is one of the most profound things I'd ever heard in my 10 years on the earth. Dewayne, with a straight face and not a hint of sarcasm nor wit, says to me,

"Well, hell, the way you kept smiling, I figured you were winning."

I look at DeWayne and, for a second, I'm furious; but then I figure I can't be mad at him, it was my fight not his. I can't live my life counting on other people to fight my battles for me. I turn to leave and find myself toppled to the ground once again. Confident it isn't an uppercut this time, I look around to see what has sent me earthward. It appears I have tripped over a random brick lying alone in the middle of the vacant lot.

Politically Detained

Malik Salaam

"Can I make you a sandwich or somethin'?"

Hussein didn't even look up. His lack of response, though, wasn't an attribute of sheer rudeness. Rather, it stemmed from an all-around intensity that concentrated on the "now moment," and the harsh fact that, at fifteen years of age, Hussein had acquired quite a skill for survival. *The darker the situation, the brighter my idea,* he often bragged.

"Hussein, are you hungry... 'Sain - I know you hear me."

Victoria was a beautiful young woman in her early twenties and stood about 5' 10." She was a complete three inches taller than the under-aged/under-privileged lad that often seemed as if he was blatantly ignoring her inside the walls of a home in which she was supposedly *the head chick in charge*. It was this sort of detachment that intrigued Victoria because those who were labeled as her peers, more often than not, became the victim of their own uncontrolled desires... Victoria was fine as cat hair. Magnificently high cheekbones. Her skin... an amazing hue of caramel that seemed to naturally glisten with flakes of bronze. Honey Brown. And although Hussein was completely entranced by the beauty that loved him uncontrollably, he was the victim of an emotional detachment that is very common amongst inner-city Black men... or outer-city... or every city, for that matter.

Victoria, on the other hand, had no way of shielding, not only, her feelings for this man-child in a land without promise, but her over all amazement for this...boy. Although his age, at times, was a factor; it had very little to do with the amazement. But Hussein's mother was convinced that Victoria was robbing her son of his innocence. Often, Victoria would answer the phone only to be greeted by the frantic ravings of a woman determined to save her son's soul. A soul that didn't need saving. No, for Victoria, the amazement was not about Sain's age. It was an emotion that she could not explain and from a place that she didn't even know existed. A place that traveled past illusion: not filled with the hypocrisy and insincerity. The place, like her feelings, was pure.

And because of this purity, Victoria was never able to see anything wrong with the love they shared. The scary truth was that Hussein was really the dominant person in the relationship. He was well read; he wrote beautiful poetry and looked into Victoria's eyes in a way that made her feel he held the only key created to unlock her soul. For Victoria, even sex had no real meaning until the night Hussein brought her to his homeboy's lavishly decorated bachelor pad, and opened her legs and her heart in a smooth, simultaneous motion.

"Naw baby, I ain't really all that hungry right now," Hussein whispered intensely, never taking his eyes off of his focal point. Often when faced with a situation that seemed to have no easy way out, Hussein would stare at a stain on the wall or a groove in the concrete until it took some type of physical form. Usually, the illusion would take shape and last just long enough for him to completely work out the problem. Tonight, it wasn't happening.

"You know what," finally breaking his trance, "I think I'm gonna get up outta here for a second, knowwha'I'msayin.' You seen my shoes, anywhere?"

Just as Hussein stood up, a knock at the door sent his heart into overdrive. Hussein knew the knock. Its tone was one of misplaced authority and danger. The knock awakened Hussein's instincts of survival. Quickly, and with as little noise as possible, Hussein gathered his belongings: a pack of Newport's, a crisp twenty dollar bill, his quarter-length hooded shearling.... *Where the fuck are my shoes.*

Some argue that the influences of intoxications make people do things that are ordinarily outside of their character. Well, Hussein often chastised himself for his bad habit of putting things in their proper places when he was extremely high – a practice that always resulted in dilemmas such as this one. He only folded his clothes or rolled his socks or hid his money when he was smoking weed. And then, the next day... Well, today was no different, and the knock on the door was becoming more impatient. Suddenly, Hussein disappeared into the bedroom and came out with his shoes, shaking his head in amusement. *Weed makes you do some strange shit.*

Sitting on the couch and lacing up his black Hi-Tech Boots (that were probably identical to the pair that was being worn by the individual on the other side of the door), Hussein signaled for Victoria to answer the door.

"Yes," Victoria cleared her throat in an attempt to wipe out any indications of suspicion, "Who is it?"

"Dekalb County Police — — open up the door, Ma'am."

Hussein knew he knew the knock. Motioning Victoria to open the door, Hussein readied himself for what was to be the start of a wild evening. Victoria slowly reached for the doorknob. Her mind was "tootsie rollin" with possibilities of what would happen once she and The Officer (Overseer/Enforcer) stood face to face. *Who had called him? Am I gonna be charged with statutory rape? Maybe they will scrape the flesh of my vagina for traces of semen? How the fuck am I gonna handle jail?* After all she was gorgeous, but she lacked any desire to be the live-in lover of some butch inmate named Maggie... *And what the fuck was Hussein doing crouched over like Jesse fuckin' Owens?*

Victoria cracked the door and peered through the opening, allowing herself ample leverage to slam the door shut... *Just in case.* "How may I help you, officer," she crooned, trying to sound as nonchalant as possible.

"Ma'am, open the door." The officer's tone was matter a fact, and Victoria realized that this was not one of those situations where her good looks and high estrogen count would work in her favor. She let out a deep sigh and took a quick glance over her shoulder. Hussein had not changed his stance. Victoria stepped back and widened the crack in the door, giving The Enforcer (Officer/Overseer) full view of the living room. Nothing special about it: a couch stained with her and Hussein's love, a black-n-gold glass coffee table, which sat on a rug embroidered with a ferocious (and supposedly sexy) black panther, one of those huge fans that all Black people hang on their walls, and...

Get the fuck outta my way!!!!

Hussein exploded past The Officer (Enforcer/Overseer) with such force that if it weren't for The Enforcer's (Overseer's/Officers) *superior combat training,* Hussein would have knocked him clear over the banister. Skipping as many steps as possible, he knew that the pursuit was on, and in order to be the victor, it was mandatory to maintain his lead. *Goddamn this muthafucka's fast.* Hussein jumped down the final four steps and broke into his almost flawless rendition of Flo Jo – back straight and arms pumping. He was so consumed with his perfected form, his mind was damn near lost in the fantasy of the 400-yard relay. *I could have run track...*

Then, reality sunk back in. His thighs were burning. His lungs were screaming. And the smell of the pig's snuff-dipping breath was burning the naps on his neck. Hussein knew the race was over. But the end had yet to be written because there was no way he was going to cave in or give up.

And then, it happened. The first thing he felt was a violent yank on his hood, followed by his body awkwardly whirling in a complete 180 degrees, and ending with his clenched fist sinking into the clammy flesh of the savage that hunted him. The chase was over, but now, the blue uniform was complimented with the fire red color of The Overseer's (Officer's/Enforcer's) neck. It is rumored that the quickest way to piss off Atlanta's finest is to actually engage them in some sort of physical activity, especially when that activity is impromptu. You see if this 6'2"-country fed-pick a nigga-lynch him for fun-badge totting-cracka had been responding to a 211 or 187 or even your typical racially profiled traffic stop, he would have had time to amp himself up for a good ole southern coon hunt. But he was just following up on your run of the mill missing black boy report. Really, the most he expected was to intimidate some young teenager who was already terrified of him, his steel black jack, and his shiny squad car (with the fancy blue lights). The pig never even expected to find a missing child at all.

Hussein, on the other hand, had no idea why the police was even there. But in his mind, his entire existence was a crime. It seemed everything he witnessed in his family and in his neighborhood gave truth to that thought. And he couldn't even fathom his mother having the audacity to call the police when she kicked him out. Other than that, the knock on the door was 12 (an Atlanta term of endearment for the pigs), and for Hussein, nothing good could ever come from that.

Although it was Hussein's first full ride in the back of a squad car, there was something strangely familiar about the experience. There was a certain emotion that seemed very common to him. To be trapped. To be isolated and alone. Thrown in the back seat and abandoned.

The ole folks have a saying: *Boy, look like yo' daddy just spit you out.* Well, the similarity between him and his mother's sperm donor reached far beyond their physical appearances. There was the strange resemblance of their personalities; so much so, a brick wall existed between Hussein and the rest of his family. This wall was as much illusionary as it was real. His mother and sisters or as his mother referred to, "me and my girls," lived in one world and he lived in another. His ride to the precinct was no different than his life. He was alone....

Hussein was jerked into the juvenile facility. Not quite what he expected. There was an extremely fat, round, white lady - who actually looked more pink than white - sitting at a desk, fingering what looked like a few stapled pieces of copy paper... although, she actually held it like it was a really important log book... *Maybe all the crew members of the Amistad.*

Hussein saw what he perceived to be four or five closet spaces with gray, metal grated doors. Then with the change of guards, he was ushered in front of one and told to: remove his shoes, belt, jewelry, beeper, money, and put them inside of the shoes. He was nudged into the closet with steel grates locked, and there it was: Hussein and three walls, one door, but no way out. He eased down on the bench and took a moment to read the prophecy chipped on the wall: *(maybe with somebody's fingernail... or the button from their pants.... or maybe..... a safety pen).* 6 POPPIN — 5 DROPPIN. EASTSIDE, BITCH. FUCK THA POLICE. RICO WAZ HERE — WHEN THE FUCK CAN HE LEAVE. And then, there was silence. Time stood still, and sleep began to overtake Hussein's already exhausted frame.

"Ey what you in here fo'?" Despite the inflections of a somewhat unnatural form of Ebonics, the voice was clearly without melanin.

Probably one of those for real ass punk rock trailer trash white boys, listenin' to Biz Markie and shit... "Who tha fuck wanna know?" *Mario-'dem always say that you betta letta nigga know you hard in Ju-vee.*

"I'm over here in the next cell. Dem mutherfuckers got me fo' shoplifting this time.... This your first time in?" The voice from inside the walls was evidently going to talk with or without Hussein's help.

"Hell naw it ain't my first time," he lied.

A brief moment of silence.

"Yeah...shiittt I've been caught for assault, possession, running away, drunken disorderly... and what am I forgetting... Oh, um, indecent exposure. So, what they git you for?"

Hussein folded his arms and closed his eyes. *The situations I find myself in are sooo fuckin' unbelievable.* Hussein thought about the absence of his father and the bitterness of his mother. He thought about Victoria who loved him because he had yet to be tarnished by a world that hated his very existence. It is an existence he would fight for as long as he walked the Earth. "I'm a political prisoner," he murmured.

Hussein couldn't have been more correct.

My Heart's Ghetto
by Amir Sulaiman

few will see me
deeply
buried in the cemetery
of my own words
or somewhere in the suburb

          of thought

I know not my inner city

my intellect is a slum lord
renting space with turning doors
glass ceilings and no floors
places where you can find rats in drawers
corners with whores
blocks where 44s
ring out in chorus
where quiet means noise
pure silence they avoid
because pure silence means danger
so the block gets paranoid

my emotions find their homes
and spend their lives
in the underprivileged, deprived
and oppressed ghettos of my mind
they settle for the kind
of dilapidated buildings surrounded by crime
emotions with too many children and not enough time
on any corners you may find
an old and neglected feeling holding a sign
saying, "I will cry for food"
and he won't get a bite or a dime
I figure it's just a matter of time
before my emotions rise up to over throw my mind

     but my intellect is not concerned
     because it is never his block that gets burned

soon ideas will appear
in riot gear
to confine the motion of emotions

and subdue the masses
but an emotion screams "down with the fascists!"
the conflict becomes inevitable
as the influence of my heart and mind clashes
the feelings are fired upon with
rubber bullets and tear gases
(my feelings don't mind
I've been trying to cry for years)
but when the smoke clears
the buildings are burned black
and manifests their worst fears
the feelings have destroyed
the homes and business of their peers
the heart is ruined
with neither light nor life
they rebuild day and night
but they are like
the blind man who regains his sight
and then closes his eyes
forever

it's a jungle sometimes it makes me wonder
how I keep from going under
don't   push   me   'cause   I'm   close   to   the   edge
I'm   trying   not   to   lose   my   hea(rt)d

Beyond This Hemisphere
by Malik Salaam

This is a poem
for those who cry
angel tears
I wonder do......angels fear for
those they guard 'til
their day of retribution
No sight set for solution

I smoke — —

lungs charred
crumbled forty acres for
restitution
because today — — was as hard as
the day before — yester/year the test of
fear
hope fades and
disappears —
                            somewhere in the twilight
could a poem shed light
on
souls that weep
my souls that keep on/keepin' on
because cities...
because cities only sleep and leave stains
on
darkened cheeks
Forgotten life reeks.........
of death
I need a chance to breathe life

        limp-n-tired

Fore I am of those forgotten,
the down trodden,
a hobbit from the shire —
The muck-n-mire
of a police zone where
chrome spins on tires

before they are snatched — —
by the chrome that spits fire......
Father forgive us —
even though, we know
exactly what we do
somehow
we are left to guess exactly what to do
Confusion — —
is this hemisphere's ultimate / alma Mata
and graduation lacks a cap and gown
Rather — —
your classmates bust
caps-n-rounds
and they toe-tag your degree and
drop your zip-lock in the ground
an attempt at levelin the playin field

They play us with desires
made to feel like
basic needs....
Made to believe
that we aren't judged by
the honor of our deeds
rather on
what
property we hold
the deed to
that is all they will ever feed you
They would prefer to
gut you open and bleed you
e.b.t.
ain't to feed you
those who despise you
will never truly feed you

Deceive our perception, we
achieve their deception

Flying colors for coloreds who
water the seedling that
uproots our roots and
branches us into picture perfect proper assimilators
who imitate
master and his whip
the tragic tale of those who

fought
for us to sit in the front row in the
wake of the wind
only to bend our backs for
the violation of our cracks and
street corners and
apartment buildings/buildings are
boarded and
burning the namesakes that they bare
and I swear to honor
the freedom that was fought for
and my heart cries
the tears of angels that
mourn the poor and
forgotten,
        down trodden

Hobbits from the shire
that survive the
muck-n-mire of this hemisphere....

G'ds angels are not meant
for the confines of this
hemisphere

You can outdistance that which is running after you but not what is running inside of you.

— Rwandan Proverb

freedom song
by Kim Caldwell

i inherited a song from long ago
wind blown breezes
that whisper wishes
set me free
master's back lashes back flip
into master's lips spitting
nigger
girl
cunt
in my ear
as he grunts and grinds
out his love for "fine nigger bitches"
i know why billie was blue
she was heir to a song
sang long before she was born
then passed it on to me
little girl lost
looking for love
god bless the child
that's got her own
freedom
billie sing me free

i inherited a song from long ago
battered and bruised beats blown on horns
that moan and mourn
trumpeting tears
that reverberate
rape
lynching
jim crow
white folks only
valaida blow
snow queen bleeds black when she's blue
and she's always blue
outfit her in pink orchids
and she is still blue
expatriate her to France
and she is still blue
place her on stage
and she blows blue

her tone is blue
she hums blue
but shines like silver lining
valaida blow free for me

i inherited a song from long ago
sashaying shimmying shaking loose demons
that dredge up my past indiscretions
indiscreetly reminding me
that i am black
and i am woman
scats scatter screams
that peel me down in layers
soft bones exposed
i can't hold up this weight
weighing me down
cut me to the meat
and i resound
blue veins display red rhythms
that rip rifts into a crescent moon child
that moans melodic muses into music
black is the color
of nina's moan
of nina's song
of the life she leads
 of the air she breathes
nina moan free into me

i inherited a song from long ago
sang and blown through blues
that blanketed my birth
passed down
from black palm to black palm
from black heart to black heart
from black eyes to black eyes
the desire for freedom pushed pride
way past the point of being strong
way past the point of where i belong
these hips mothered your earth
these lips kissed concentrated courage
and painted pain into picture perfect
i never learned my place
i inherited a freedom song
my freedom song
is your freedom song

is their freedom song

Room to Breathe

Kim Caldwell

It is once again 3:00 a.m. and like clockwork, she rises. Not because she has to prepare herself for work. That's not for another four hours. And not because the baby's crying – she miscarried two years ago. And not because he was tossing and turning, he left months ago. She has an entire list of reasons why she shouldn't be up at 3:00 a.m., but here she is, again. And she knows exactly what needs to be done. She gets dressed and grabs her keys. She locks the door behind her and steps out into the comfort of the still, dark night. As she walks towards her car, she fades into the darkness. She gets in and starts the engine. Immediately, she is comforted by the gentle idle of the engine. She is comforted by the anonymity that comes with being just another person on the highway. So, she drives towards that comfort.

Here she is, again, traveling the city highways. More than traveling, she's thinking while driving, but more so...driving to free herself. There is something about the steady hum of the engine that lulls her, calms her, and opens the bridge to her thoughts - and usually, the dam to her tears. There is safety in the blackness right before dawn... hope on the horizon. The highway releases her from her loneliness. There is always someone else traveling with her. Maybe there is more purpose in their reasoning – probably less emotion; but, she is guaranteed to see other cars on the road. Either way, she is never alone on the highway – not like when she is at home. The quiet of the house overwhelms her. It beats her down until she's cowering in the corner of the sofa; her head smashed face first into her pillow. The silence covers her with reminders of her losses... her lost childhood, her lost baby, and her lost life. There is something about succumbing to the blackness of the night, which allows her room to breathe. Most times, that is all she needs – room to breathe.

She doesn't bother to turn on the radio. Her thoughts provide the score to this scene. Her eyes are puffy and red with tears that barely leak from her eyelids. Headlights from cars traveling in other directions, to other places, to other people, with other thoughts, flash across her face. She catches a glimpse of herself in the rearview mirror and the tears are freed from the dam that has been holding them at bay. She cries fiercely, repeating over and over again, "How did I get here again?" She retraces her yesterday, her last week, her last month, her last year and finds that she is recycling her desperation. She is desperate to stop in mid-flight, but she doesn't know how. She is desperate to cry out, but she doesn't know how. She is desperate to beg for help, but she doesn't know how. She is desperate to leave this life, but doesn't know how to stop living. She is hoping, more than hoping - needing someone to question her well-being. She needs someone to question her 3:00 a.m. drives and the thoughts that drove her to them. She needs someone to ask what is on her mind, what is ailing her heart, and stifling her soul. What is killing her spirit? She needs someone to see past her finely tuned façade and into the turmoil brewing inside of her. She hopes that she will crack under the pressure of being a "strong, black woman" in front of a room full of people, so that her weakness becomes undeniable. So that everyone has no choice but to pull her down from her pedestal, brush her off, and let her cry out loud. Let her breathe through her misery.

Does she even possess the capacity to breath? Can she be honest about the space she resides in? Wasn't she afraid of exposing her shaky foundation? Why else would she find comfort in the darkness of 3:00 a.m. drives when passersby's won't have the opportunity to feign concern? They are unable to see through the night into the darkness clouding her heart. Why else would she mute her moans under the spray of the shower behind drawn curtains? Never openly crying out... never outwardly showing need. Life had taught her that no one wants to hear the moans or see the contorted face of another black woman crying about lost time, lost lives, lost children. So she drove to save everyone's sympathy-laden sentences for someone who could use them. She had no use for sympathy.

It's much easier on the souls of others that she maintains the image of "having it together" because they were ill-equipped to handle her falling apart. They would never be able to muster the strength to piece her back together – to make her whole again – if she took the liberty of falling apart right before their eyes. Besides, she had been pulled apart so long ago, she had gotten used to the feeling. She would not even be able to recognize her whole self. She left pieces scattered throughout her life. Her father carried a piece of her in his pocket. Like loose change, he never used it, but liked the comfort of the sound. Her mother carried a piece of her like a key that unlocks a secret door to her mind. She had lost a piece of herself in relationships come and gone. She had miscarried a baby who carried away incongruent pieces of her heart. She had purposely discarded pieces of her past to fit snugly into her picture perfect present. She had never really seen herself whole.

She was driving and crying. She was searching the pavement for the lost pieces. She desperately needed to reach herself, so she grasped the wheel and exceeded beyond speeds of 95 mph. She was hoping the police would pull her over and demand to know where the fire was so she could tell them that the fire was inside and she was trying to put it out - dying to put it out. She wanted to explain that she was running from herself to herself. She wanted someone to stop her and ask why was she driving so recklessly. She wanted them to ask her where she was headed. So she accelerated, hoping that she would run into a police speed trap. But there were none. She was trapped with this fire burning inside of her. She needed to put it out or die. So she did. That night, she lost control of the car...of herself and hit the median wall. The impact activated the airbags, breaking her neck and instantly killing her. She never took a breath, but finally found room to breathe.

Now and Then
by Amir Sulaiman

I see a piece of a man
blinking slowly
talking quickly
but he's alone and lonely
his eyes hit me
(does he know me?)
he's past tipsy
something told me
to listen closely
I stopped in my tracks then he approached me
he smelled mostly
of cheap scotch
he had a gold watch
that didn't tick
how ridiculous!
that's when he moved even more closely
he reached in his coat and unfolds these
sheets of loose leaf
of poems that he hadn't finished composing
as his mouth was opening
his eyes were closing
he said…

the reality is
you love fantasy
I prefer the reality of confusion
to the seduction of illusion
so I understand that we last
shortly
we are tiny
and our time is near
so what else is there

> *except to be*
> *sincere*

my peers appear to be dead
or are yet to be born
or perhaps they have not yet
been loved by the norm
and adored by the norm
then bored by the norm
then burned and scorned by the norm

people are

funny

fickle

and dying

our time is near
                    so what else is there
                        except to be
sincere
in a child's first year it's in search of it's third year
in it's tenth year it's in search of it's sixteenth year
in a it's fiftieth it's in search of it's twenty-fifth year
and when it's dead it is in search of it's life
why should it not be in search of Now
you don't even have to search for Now
Now is here
has Now used you and abused you
maybe Now loves you and doesn't want to lose you
what if something accused you
of not being good enough when it just met you
you hardly know Now
in the same way you desire then Now
              you will desire Now then
so, it seems, you are searching for what is present

as he finished he gently folded the poem in half
stuck out is other dirty palm and asked
for a couple dollars
I gave him the cash
he turned his collar
as we passed
and returned to his spot
a half block up the ave.

We live in strange days
you'll find the truth in many strange ways
just keep your soul close cope and maintain
some of those most deranged are really the best at staying sane

MASTECTOMY
by Jon Goode

And she was the definition of beauty
She was tall
She was completely bald
She was Fresh out of recovery
From her mastectomy
Being a breast amputee
Made her no less of a woman to me
Those lumps of flesh across her chest simply made breasts
But breasts have never made a woman and breast never made she
And she
Held her head high
With a sense of peace in her eyes
That could not be denied
And could not be described or explained if I tried
Sustained by her sense of faith
And her sense of pride
As she began to walk
You could sense it in her stride
She stuck out her chest and dared your eyes to not notice
That the disappearing act was fact and not some hocus pocus
That's how I happened to hear what she said to a man who came near
to offer his condolences
She said I want you to understand and please know this
"Yes,
I've second guessed
God and at times asked him why
And yes
Alone in the dark
I've oft times cried
But when my eyes are blessed to greet a new day
I understand that I have to live at least two days, today
And I understand that in someway
This is all in God's plan
So I've laid my burdens down
And taken up God's hand
Because when the chemo goes long
And I'm not so sure I can go on
God gives me a shoulder I can lean and rely on
And when I don't want no more Ensure
And I'm not so sure I can endure no more

And I fall to the floor
Not wanting to die but not truly understanding what I'm living for
Not understanding who I am
Not understanding what am I to do
That's when God takes me in his arms and he carries me through
And yes,
People love comparing me to
The strong and the brave
From Ali to MLK
But what I do is not brave
Because I just like they
Do what I have to do
Step in my Dr. Scholls
And you'll see neither my shoes nor my soul
Have walked an easy road
But I remember bein' told
It's the path you choose
But the path that chose you
The same quandary faced Luke, Mark, John and Mathew
So I laugh at those who view
This as a tragedy
It seems sad you see
But I used to live the life of Sadducees
So don't be sad for me
This had to be
Sometimes the buildings destroyed in catastrophes
Were simply blocking some things you had to see
And right now let me
Clear up some of the fallacies associated with my malady
Tho' the chemo leaves me weak
My soul is so complete
That even when I can't speak
You can see, feel and hear me through my smile
And when this earthly host is gone
And my ghost is carried home
Then I'll live on through a poem
And be reborn as a child floating down the Nile
Though I may have Cancer
Cancer will never have me
Bald with one breast
I am more and no less
Than any woman you will ever see
I am Yesterday,
I am tomorrow
I am Now and forever me

I have never asked anyone to pity or revel me
I never asked for your pardon or revelry
My mind is more concerned with the current turns taken in society
Just the other week I saw the passion of Christ on a movie screen
Saw his pain depicted in some very moving scenes
But if I can't find the passion of Christ in everyday Human beings
Then 300 million in tickets sales…what does it all mean
Please understand that infants, these seeds we've sown
Will grow into little visions of we
My trial and tribulations have shown it's so much bigger than me
I'm trying to see these acorns
Grow into bigger and better trees.
And I'd give the other breast if I thought it'd help you see and believe."
And on that note she turned to me
Gave a smile and took her leave.
And she
Was oh so Beautiful.

-

Fear Nothing

Yaminah Ahmad

She stands with her feet grounded in the hardwood floor. She stands tall with her arms behind her back and hands tightly gripping one another. Her spine is straight, running parallel alongside her legs. And with her bare feet, she begins to rock back and forth, shifting her weight from her toes to her heels. The swaying causes the arches in her feet to squeak against the polished wood. The rhythm of this balancing act has her entranced and she forgets the darkness. She forgets the city lights are out and her entire neighborhood is swallowed up by blackness. She just stands in the middle of her living room, listening to the squeaking and cracking, while drowning out fear's whispers.

Hoping to get a glimpse of light, she very quickly opens and shuts her eyes. She opens her eyes and stretches them with her brows and cheekbones. Her eyes are wide open... she sees nothing. Fear begins to whisper again. When one opens their eyes, they expect to see – see something. They expect to see anything. She sees nothing. She expects to see something... she sees nothing. With every attempt, she knows she will see nothing because fear tells her that she will see nothing. But she desperately wants to see something –anything …nothing. Fear starts to whisper louder.

She shuts her eyes and begins humming to herself. The sound is virtually undetectable, but it resonates loudly in her throat. The hum creates a vibration; and although she can barely hear it, her vibrating throat eases her worries. Because the hum lives in her throat, she has to imagine what it sounds like, so her mind remembers her grandmother's hum. She smiles in the darkness. No one can see it, but she smiles. She is happy because she remembers her grandmother. The vibration in her throat conjures the memory of her grandmother. She feels safe now. Her grandmother is here in the dark.

She hears her grandmother loud and clear. Her throat vibrates and her heart beats. The beats are drums intensifying the vibrations. The beats pound against her chest, up to her throat and out of her mouth. The vibrations are words. She hears her grandmother's words. They are loud and clear. She is listening and so is fear.

Her grandmother tells her to move out of the darkness. Her grandmother tells her there is light a few yards ahead. She feels her throat vibrating and her drums beating. Her grandmother tells her the light is waiting for her outside her bedroom window. All she has to do is walk to her bedroom. She will see the moonlight shining for her. Her grandmother is loud and clear. Her throat is vibrating and her drums are beating against her chest. She smiles again, remembering the beautiful sight from many past moonlit nights. She quickly opens her eyes. Suddenly, her grandmother's voice is gone and the drumbeats fade away. She sees something, but it should be nothing. She sees something and she wished it were nothing. She sees fear.

She stares into the darkness. Her feet are firmly smashed against the hardwood floors. Her body is frozen still. She has her eyes open and she is staring at fear. Her mind tells her eyes she sees something, so her eyes say it is staring at fear. Her mind tells her eyes it sees shapes. It sees shapes forming into a figure. Fear is now someone, some body standing in front of her.

She is not alone. Her eyes are wide open and she sees Fear. Her mind tells her eyes Fear is looking back at her. Fear is looking at her, assessing her. Fear is looking at her, assessing her and drawing conclusions. Fear is forming an opinion about her. She fears its thoughts. What is Fear thinking? Fear knows her fears. She knows Fear knows her fears. She is fearful of that. Fear knows something and she knows nothing. She is powerless. And Fear knows that as well.

She stands with her feet on the hardwood floor. She stands with her arms to her side and her hands bald up in a fist. She stands with her head bowed down, avoiding Fear's constant gaze. But whether her eyes are open or closed, she still sees Fear. Fear is all around her. Fear lives inside her. There is no squeaking or cracking. No words or drumbeats. She stands with her feet on the hardwood floor in silence. The moon is shining brightly from her bedroom window. Her grandmother hums in the wind.

Foundation
by Jon Goode

I wonder if it was a man or a woman
That funded the foundation
That founded foundation
So that women all across this nation
Can cover up the pain, betrayal and lies.
I've come to realize
That a wide array of designer Shades
Are often used to hide blackened eyes from display
And Lipstick just the right shade
Can disguise and mimic healthy lips once they've been split
And blush done just right
Keeps
Bruises on cheeks
Out of sight for weeks
Get the foundation to blend in with your skin tone
And no one will begin to know the wars you wage at home
The open sores created behind closed doors
No one would suppose the hell you just been through
Everyday Women
With battle scars hidden
Conduct business as usual
Sittin' in your cubicle
Your eyes stare at the screen
And your mind replays the scenes
That seem to be
Happenin' more frequently
Seekin' the answers to the question
"Why is the man I love mistreating me?"
"Why is the man I married beating me?"
And you think back to what once
Was just a playful childish push
Has evolved into a full grown punch
Thoughts interrupted by a co-worker
Who asks you out to lunch.
You politely decline, "Nah girl not this time,"
And you flash a fake everything is fine smile
While inside your soul begins slowly crying
And Inside your soul continues slowly dying
Leaving you relying on Foundation

To support this house of lies
As you eyes stare @ the screen
And your mind replays scenes
That seem to be
Happenin' more frequently
Just the other week in the
Kitchen you limpin'
From a deep bruise
Eyes water as you kiss your daughter
And send her off to school
...like your mother used to do you
and abuse your mother
Is what your father used to do too,
Like your husband does you
It's almost as if your mother was you.
Your stories so similar
They blend into a blur
I mean you learned your make-up secrets from her
In many situations in more than one way
Mothers lay the foundation
And lot of girls grow up thinking It's OK then
And it's just that way and
When their husbands start pouring punches
Some women never say when
That's when your girlfriend comes back in your cube again
Asking if you're sho' 'cause she's about to go
You say "Nah go 'head girl I'm gone make do,"
Then you begin to think, you know what?
She wears her shades inside a lot too
And her foundation blends in with her skin so beautiful
And you begin to notice this trend from cubicle to cubicle
On the train, in the store, no matter what you do
You see a nation full of women goin' through it just like you do
And if it's the last thing you do
You'll make sure your daughter doesn't inherit the secret from you
The secret that
A wide array of designer Shades
Are often used to hide blackened eyes from display
And Lipstick just the right shade
Can disguise and mimic healthy lips once they've been split
And blush done just right
Keeps
Bruises on cheeks
Out of sight for weeks
Get the foundation to blend in with your skin tone

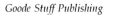

And no one will begin to know the wars you wage at home
No one would suppose the kind of foundation
Your relations are built on
The foundation of abuse.

Uncomfortably Comfortable

Daneea Badio

The darkness felt comfortable, in an uncomfortable kind of way, as she lay still, waiting for the blink to be over. After what seemed like thirty minutes, probably more like five, she decided to relinquish the remote control, roll off the bed and feel her way toward the bathroom where she kept candles, with ready matches, beside her garden tub. As she slowly shuffled her feet to avoid any accidental toe stubs, she contemplated if she'd be able to do her customary bedtime reading by candlelight. Her eyes were already strained, actually downright exhausted, from a long day of number crunching. So she wasn't sure they were up for reading anyway, but especially, not by candlelight. How could her eyes, arms and legs be so fatigued, while her mind had already weighed in for a marathon bout against the sleep warden? This was a night she really needed her late night TV, talk radio, or something or somebody to distract her from thoughts. She found herself literally praying, "Please, Dear Precious Lord, let the power please come back on," so her thoughts wouldn't tell her bedtime stories.

As she reached for the candle, she heard a thump from the bedroom. "Oh, it was just the TV," she quickly reminded herself. She could never understand why the television made those final thumping sighs after you turn it off, like it was gasping for its final breath. Or maybe it thought by abruptly interrupting your silence, it could convince you it'd be better if you turned it back on. Whatever the case, this time the thump made her jump, which for some reason, changed her course as she shuffled quicker, this time, back through the bathroom. Something in her head told her to just return to her bed and be still in the darkness. Still, in her comfortable, yet in an uncomfortable kind of way, darkness.

Shuffling back toward the bed, she momentarily detoured to slip off her pants and then her blouse, replacing her bra with a nightshirt she kept on the chair in the corner. As she walked back through the room, she didn't shuffle this time. Now, feeling more familiar with her dark space, she walked to the door and closed it, just for peace of mind, of course. From time to time, she would close her bedroom door, as a precaution, when she was feeling a little anxious about living alone. She'd told herself if someone got in the house while she was sleeping, they would have to open her door before they could get to her. The creaking door would alert her and bide her some time to grab the baseball bat she kept beneath her bed. Although she wasn't a scary person, she considered this one little step a reasonable safety measure.

"Okay, enough with this silence!" her thoughts erupted as she reached for the phone, which was also singing its own sighing song. Some cordless phones with dying batteries are quick to beg you to save them, with an annoying every two-minute "remember me" beep! "The darkness isn't so bad, but this silence is a real problem," her irritated thoughts insisted. She unplugged the phone, walked to the closet, and buried its lingering beeps under some blankets. "Don't get comfortable, maybe you can go outside, talk to your neighbors or something," the voice in her head continued. She looked out the window into more silent darkness. But she didn't know her neighbors. She barely even saw them, before or after, her 16-hour days at the office.

So she tried thinking of a familiar song to hum to herself as filler for the void of quietness. But the only one that flooded in her mind was his song, *"How do we keep the music playing, how do we make it last…"* Instantly, the heaviness in her eyes, arms and legs, rushed to her heart and the darkness seemed to creep inside her. She dropped to the bed, hips, back, shoulders and then, her head. Her left arm gently encircled her head as her right hand found a resting place on her chest. Her eyes began to fill with sorrow, then frustration; but it was her anger that forbade her heart to cry. It had been seven months since they broke up and she decided to be over it in absolutely no more than two. It was nobody's fault this time; it was a unanimous decision. Who says amicable break- ups are easier? At least when somebody's screwed up, there's someone to blame and a target for your anger. But in a case like this, where he was a good guy and she was a good girl, but good just wasn't good enough – how the hell do you blame or hate or rationalize or understand what all this craziness is really supposed to mean? Why is life so damn complicated? She admitted, only to herself, that she wasn't missing him. She missed the idea and the reality of being with someone, not alone, unattached, single. She didn't even like the word. Single. It sounds lonely…ill, like a polite plague.

Suddenly, she realized she felt one with the darkness. Both were void. And no matter how you fill up the space, it all looks the same, like unrecognizable nothingness. A diamond is no different from a rock in the dark and when it came to relationships, Jazzine felt completely in the dark. She was confident and assertive in all other aspects of her life. But when it came to love, she'd gotten it wrong so many times. She felt she had no point of reference from which to measure. She knew, in her head, she was beyond brave to have agreed to end it with Allen. She concurred with her best friend that many women would have settled for comfort in lieu of loneliness. But what's worse than feeling lonely when you're not alone? Well, maybe feeling lonely when you are alone. But at least you'd have someone to divert your attention from your loneliness, right? Well, Jazzine couldn't say that she ever really felt lonely when she was with Allen. But she knew she didn't feel the way she wanted to feel when they were together. She didn't experience excitement, anticipation or passion. And when they were apart, she never really missed him. Even now, she missed the company of companionship more than she missed him.

So now, she lay on the bed with that song, which called to her everywhere she turned after they broke up. So she coined it his song. *"How do you keep the song from fading too fast..."* And although it saddened her to hear it, it also offered approval of her decision. She knew if she and Allen's relationship didn't start off strong, there was little chance for longevity. So she knew she made the right decision, but that didn't make it an easy one. They liked each other and enjoyed each other's company. But honestly, at best, they would have been good friends, but not best friends. Except by default, which always leaves room for Devon or David or Bill, to become the source of a better connection, a flirting relationship and typically, a regretful affair years down the road.

Jazzine didn't like this path of her thoughts, so she considered her cell phone for a moment. But she didn't have the energy to get up and check to see if it was working. She felt as if a huge weight had her pinned to the bed. And so, she abandoned her contemplation and continued her journey deeper into her comfortable darkness.

"So, are you lonely?" she asked herself. Without hesitation, she instantaneously answered, "No! I have a full life, rewarding work, good friends, a great family and a comfortable existence. It's nowhere near perfect, but it is a life lots of people would die for. To be lonely would be almost ungrateful," she declared to herself. "There are too many people with real problems, experiencing real loneliness, for me to get in that line. And what is loneliness, anyway? It's feeling sorry for yourself, wishing you had someone to help you feel complete. That's definitely not me. I am completely at peace with myself and who I am. No, I'm not perfect, but I am a good, honest, attractive, intelligent woman. I just wish I had someone who could recognize and appreciate all that I am and love me for me!" She heard herself cry out loud, "Dear God... Why can't I find someone to love who really loves me? Is that too much to ask? I know a lot of awful, dishonest, unattractive, disrespectful people who get to have meaningful or, at least, sustainable relationships and here I am alone??!! Okay, what am I supposed to learn from this and can we get this class over with before I turn 100? Enough is enough already! "

Now she was sitting up on the bed, propelled forward by her backward evaluations of everybody else's life in comparison to hers. The darkness, which had settled into vague shapes, began to again lose its clarity as her contemplations grew more and more cloudy. Why do we automatically lash out at the innocent bystanders when we feel under attack, or to be more accurate, exposed? Must our truth shine its light on everybody else's dark corners to serve our need for equal disclosure? That was a horrible thing to think and even worse to say out loud. "Awful, dishonest, unattractive, disrespectful people..." Jazzine began thinking, who am I to judge? Why can't they have "meaningful or at least sustainable relationships?" Because guess what? They're just people, just like everybody else with our imperfect, flawed, unbalanced, and sinful ways. And I'm sure none of their relationships exist without their own set of challenges that only they could know. Because nobody really knows what's going on in a relationship but the two people involved and sometimes only one of them is really in on the complete story. How many of us find out years later that our own parents' relationships weren't what they seemed? And that's in a house we, ourselves, lived in daily. So how dare I compare or try to conclude anything about anyone else's character or worthiness for happiness.

That's one, among many things, that's really cool about God. He considers nearly all sins equal, whether lying or cheating or stealing, He doesn't rank and rate sin the way we do. Given a different set of circumstances, who's to say what each of us is really capable of doing or saying or being. Jazzine was reminded about the way her girlfriends would rant and rave about another girlfriend's relationship woes. They were quick to announce, "I don't know why she puts up with him" or "She's a good one, I would never..." But truth be told, every one of them had endured their own worse case scenarios and would probably suffer through them again. Especially if they showed up in an attractive package, cleverly disguised as something other than the same old mess.

"But my truth is, I don't have time to feel lonely," she heard herself think to herself. But those words got caught in repeat mode: "I don't have time to feel lonely. I don't have time to feel lonely. I don't have time to feel. I don't have time to...feel?" Jazzine began to ponder. Had she, in fact, medicated her loneliness and possibly other feelings with her drugs of choice - a hectic, demanding, self important and overly committed life? She acknowledged that even her downtime was strictly scheduled.

She permitted herself to recline back onto the bed, as her even breathing continued to sing his song's melody. *"How do you lose yourself to someone and never lose your way..."* Had she lost herself to this recreation of herself? How much of who she was did she really want to be or had consciously chosen to be? Was she happy - cheerful and joyful? Or was she content - satisfied and comfortable?

And the song continued to dance about her room... *"The more I love the more that I'm afraid, that in your eyes I may not see forever..."* Had she, in her unconscious deliberation, chosen men she could not love, because then she wouldn't have to rely on them for her forever? Maybe she'd chosen the men who would, in a strange way, stroke her ego by proving her right about them, even at the expense of her heart. She never really remembered being surprised by any of her relationship outcomes. Her intuition, as obvious as it may have been to everyone else, was always "right again!" She had to admit she was more often concerned with being correct in her assessment of the relationship than she was with being hurt by their failures.

As she tallied her short list in her head, she found an undertone of pride. She had been right about Wilbert, who was too consumed and married to his business to really love anyone else. Although, he did get married within a year of their breakup...*obviously to some shallow girl with no life of her own.* "Oops! There I go again!" Rebuking her disapproving judgments, she continued. She also had Sam all figured out. He was just too good looking, with his fine self, to settle for just one charm on his arm. He had to have it, at least until he got it, and then it was on to the next conquest. So she knew almost from the start that she could never allow herself to feel secure in that relationship. Maybe she too had to have it until she got it. Maybe so she too could say, she had had it. He was really something special, in every way! She had to confess she had no regrets. Sam was great for the few months they lasted. And she'd been right about Jeffrey and Vince too. Even Allen was too nice a guy to complement or contend with her craziness. And so it went, each time she'd uncover their imperfections, she would eject them and affirm herself as the wiser for it.

But now, as she lay in her comfortable darkness, she asked herself, "Could I be the problem?" Again she promptly replied "No! I'm not getting sucked into that crazy self analysis everybody gets hung up on. It's not me. There's absolutely nothing wrong with me. I have my everyday issues just like everybody else, but I'm no special basket case or charity case or case in point for lonely women everywhere! And when are these damn lights gonna come back on anyways!"

Jazzine raised herself off the bed, pushing through the invisible weight that had previously overpowered her. She made her way to the bathroom to use it, more as a diversion than out of necessity. She found her way to the sink to wash her hands and splash her face, when she remembered she had failed to wash off her day's make-up. She felt her way to the Noxema, located her make-up washcloth, and began her cleansing regimen. Jazzine thought about those other women in her office who wore tons of make-up. What were they trying to cover up? Who were they really? She never got that heavy into make up. She never got into to much of anything that became too time consuming, like elaborate hair styles, flawless wardrobe coordination, or layers of make up. A little mascara, eyeliner and a touch of shine on her lips were all the beauty exercises she was willing to do.

She began to calculate. How many of those overly made up women had men? If she believed what they told her, every last one of them had at least one man. Most had more. Maybe men are more attracted to illusions than they are to the... What am I saying? Of course they are!! Men drool over those perfect supermodel types. They love long hair, supple breasts and big round butts and would do almost anything to have the honor of banging any woman possessing one or more of their dream beauty butt and breast combinations.

"So, maybe that's my problem," she thought. "Maybe I'm too obsessed with the search for authenticity." Let's face it. How many people are really in touch with who they are, anyways? Did she even really know who she was? She began to analyze the person she had become. Was the person she presented to the world really authentic? Or just someone she had created and could therefore control more so than the flawed person she really was? Surprisingly, Jazzine felt a smile breaking through her comfortable darkness, which now felt like a warm hug enveloping her, as she took gliding steps on her way back from the bathroom. She returned to the bed to lay with her eyes closed in anticipation, as she asked herself, "Who have I become? How much of who I am is who I really want to be? And why do I run from my own thoughts?"

She was determined to be still in the safety of her comfortable darkness as she unleashed her discomforting thoughts. "Why do I run from my thoughts? What truth or analysis am I unwilling to confront?" Then she released it, like a clutch released prematurely, making the car jolt forward. Out loud, she uttered, "What if I never find anyone to love me?"

And then she answered, "How can I, if I never allow anyone to know...me." Even with Allen, she remembered holding herself back. She was afraid to reveal the fullness of herself. She thought it would be too overwhelming for him. He was such a nice, quiet, reserved kind of guy. Or was he? Maybe he was pretending too. And with every man she'd ever dated, she'd hid the part of herself she thought would drive him away. Yet they left anyway. So maybe she did drive them away, after all. Because she really never liked to deal with anything that was too time consuming. She walked cautiously through relationships to avoid even an accidental toe stub, not to mention getting her heart bruised. The closed doors to her heart were kept closed to allow time to reinforce her boundaries, if someone got close while her guards were sleeping. And although, in her head, she really believed she wanted each relationship to last, she had to acknowledge, she'd usually feel a sigh of relief after it was over. But maybe it was a fluttering attempt to convince her that, for once, she should try to stick it out. And in the pages and scripts of her bedtime stories, she never found the answers to the questions she was determined not to ask. And so now in her comfortable darkness, she began to see clearly. Fear of failure had steered her straight to her point of concentration. She could never get around the tree in the middle of the road, because she was so busy staring at it, concentrating so hard on avoiding it, until it consumed her field of vision - causing her to ram right into it, every time.

Now, as she opened her eyes feeling the moonlight illuminating her room, she arose from the bed to adjust her blinds, only to notice her clock flashing 12:36 a.m. in the opposite corner of the room. She chuckled to herself and continued humming her song... "*I know the way I feel for you is now or never...*" And in that moment she vowed to choose now over never. She would live now, open herself to new possibilities, and try her hand at loving. As she made her way to start a moonlit bath, she reconciled, in her mind, that loneliness is not an awful curse. It is a gift. It's an opportunity for self-analysis and a chance to define your own sense of completeness. She would guess that few people would actually accomplish this great quest while in a relationship. Surely most would opt against this taxing, often painful journey of self-discovery. But eventually, she surmised, most of us are destined to walk this path. Some go, forced by a major change in their life, like an illness, or a significant death or divorce. Not until then, do they come to the realization that they're really not in touch with themselves.

Although, she'd only just begun her journey, she knew she was in the place she needed to be. In her comfortable darkness, she could reveal every part of herself and it would all look the same, unranked and unrated. But more than anything she would turn her attention to the life she wanted most. No more avoiding the tree in the middle of the road. Now she'd focus her attentions on that funky house on the hill, with the sounds of cheerful music playing, and children skipping about the porch. That's the new vision she'd hone in on. She would neither carelessly maneuver through life nor warily seek to control every step either. Just beyond her now clear path, through the darkness, she knew there was so much more her God was preparing her for. She only had to demonstrate her faith and readiness to receive it.

Vagabond
by Amir Sulaiman

Loneliness keeps me company when I'm alone
and most times that is enough
often I need no home
the soul's rolling stone
a vagabond
roaming the mind's country side
robbing the settlers of their thoughts
the sun has darkened my neck
the dust has darkened my shoes
I am a drifter having
occasional
passionate
short-lived
romances
with the common ideas
of the common folk

but when I'm still

I can feel my internal
inferno
burning for the companionship of words
I stand on the edge of something
looking into the depths of nothing
this is where I find
myself
my test
and inspiration
I wouldn't call it a meditation
more like a conversation
simply an opening of one's self to one's self
it is to undress
the ugliness of last year
the progress of the present
it is to dig in the graveyard of your youthful aspirations
and excavate the decaying carcass of your ideal

I am not a hero
and I am going to die soon

so I may never be a hero
and die the death of regular men
this compels me to the road again
running from home
to home
and back again

my friends are abstract
ideas I entertain
my home is a place
I must've seen but can't explain
I'm passing my time
passing for sane
passing the blame
left of myself
but right to my name
but my only defense are these abstract
ideas I entertain
my home is a place
I must've seen but can't explain
I know that I've been home
and that I've felt once
in some memory
at some place
in my distant youth
I cried tenderly
loved intensely
But now
I don't think that my feelings remember me
my heart feels filled with November leaves
tumbled by a December breeze
April may never come
the groundhog stays underground
with no desire to see the sun
I am a vagabond
not a fugitive so
I don't live on the run

I live on a walk

the type of slow stroll
that gives one
some time to think
some time to breath
just some time to get away from things

but I never come back to things
and forget the things I was getting away from
                                        and why

perhaps my things have died
under my bed
or instead
they are building strength
in the dark cloud over my head
perhaps they won't come to light
until I'm older (or dead)
I remind me of what this loner once said
"no one needs anyone"
and I believed him
but who wants to lead the non-life that he led
I wasn't born alone
my mother was there
and I won't die alone
the angel of death will be there
but I will be alone before Allah
when my book of deeds is disclosed
when my sins are exposed
that dark part of my heart
        that nobody knows
I won't have the comfort of company
not even the comfort of clothes

I stand naked and nervous before Truth

I am not a hero
and I am going to die soon
so I may never be a hero
and die the death of regular men
this compels me to the road again
running from home
to home
and back again
I am vagabond

A Whisper Lies

Malik Salaam

At one in the morning, there is not a whole lot of time for frivolous thoughts. Whispers found missing in the darkness of the building's shadow ... suddenly broken... Rasheed's heart skipped a half beat... His eyes searched for the source of abrupt violation. Despite the glow, he knew it wasn't the cocaine white '79 Cutlass Supreme. Drop top. A mutter of success: success Rasheed longed for. There was no car; it was only the red light of a business sign that snatched him from the daze of his thoughts

The red glare was a beacon that alerted the world: hot dough had just leaped from grease, bathed in glaze, and lay waiting and warm. Rasheed stared at the crimson glow. He thought about how Keisha would react if he opened the door surprisingly carrying the large flat box. Somewhere in his mind he wondered if it would make up for the fact that his trip was, yet again, financially unsuccessful. Almost a whisper...

See, that's why I don't be fuckin' with these niggas, his thoughts hissed. And right on key, the white walls scratched the sidewalk and NWA hummed in with the crickets and the inner-city sounds of the West End. "'Bout time," Rasheed mumbled to himself.

The driver of The Classic locked eyes with him, slightly cocking his jaw upward and to the right. Rasheed wondered why Brothas always put their chin towards the sky when they were greeting one another, but it certainly appeared that even when delivered with the greatest of confidence, they still meekly nodded towards their historical master. Face down. *Probably 'cause we scared...* Rasheed shunned the idea of intimidation and shook the whisper off, scratching his beard for comfort. He also understood the power of things passed on from generations. His life was dedicated to painting that pain and coloring it with the beauty of a new legacy. He wanted his paintings to spark change. He was hell bent on... Rasheed decided to postpone the contemplation of his fate until after his transaction.

"What's happenin' wit' it," Rasheed asked, lowering his window and adjusting his demeanor. "What the bi'ness?"

"Shit... same big bowl of it," the voice's tone carried a southern drawl that led Rasheed to believe he encountered a kindred soul that shared some of the same ideals. The voice came from another member of a small community that yearned and struggled, not always unwavering, but mostly, consistent towards something... anything that existed as more than an arrogant murmur. For most people, it was a life that lacked substance. The twang also reminded him that he was back in Atlanta and for Rasheed, it was always good stuff to connect with kin-folk after a couple of weeks on the road.

The two veterans smiled and greeted each other with a hand-shake, forty dollars, and eight grams of mid-grade marijuana all in one flawless motion.

"No doubt..."

"Fa'sho'..."

"How was the road?"

"Nigga – glad to be back in the A."

"Shiiittt... throw your boy a hundred..." Closing with a couple of smiles and another exchange of dap, they reached completion. Rasheed admired the two navy blue racing stripes running parallel on the trunk and briefly gazed at the brake lights as the voice peeled off. He began to plan his route to his front door... the route that would be filled with the least police spottings possible... He turned the keys dan-gling in the ignition.

The clicking sound from under the hood informed Rasheed that Keisha's starter had become another outstanding debt.

Rasheed triple-checked to make sure the vehicle's doors were locked and his collection of five CDs was safe. *Last thing I need is for anything in this moafucka to get took.* He pictured Keisha exiling her nor-mal laid back demeanor to flail her arms in disgust about her car break-ing down and being left abandoned in the parking lot – only to be van-dalized thanks to Rasheed's inability to get the starter fixed months ago. In his head he tried to imagine the venom from her screams, but they sounded more like annoying whispers. He paid no attention to the 'No Parking' sign. He patted the outside of his pocket to make sure the small package was secure...

Rasheed remembered - *hot doughnuts*, and made his way to the front entrance.

The shop's bright fluorescents bounced off the cream tiles and forest green vinyl seats. Quickly sculpting the corners of his mouth, Rasheed flared his nostrils, furrowed his brow, but his eyes... danced happily across the sheet pans on the cooling racks.

His desire posed seductively in dozens, and he craved for the warm sugar and grease to stick to his fingerprints. He listened as the sweet glaze whispered for him to buy them by the caseload, forgetting the sharp pain that was created when the sugar took root in his decay-ing teeth. The chipped filling and cavities... Cavities which were more like craters... The ruin remains of nerve endings from where molars had actually rotted out of his mouth. Nonetheless, he pushed the shrill of discomfort out of his mind's reach, dismissed the incident as a gift for Keisha and purchased a baker's dozen. *Gotta have one for the road.* Rasheed watched the counter clerk prepare his package. Arranging his desires into the three rows of four or four rows of three, depending on how you looked at it in the flat box.

"Baby, you can just put the extra one in a napkin."

She didn't respond, not even her eyes spoke a word. Rasheed thought about how disappointing it must be to live one's life trapped in dead ends. Jobs and relationships – void of options. An entire nation. For that brief moment, he found solace in his dreams... a peace that was rarely present in the wake of an overwhelming, immediate reality. The small top, large bottom woman handed Rasheed the box without words, turned on the flats of her arches, and allowed her hands to sink into her hips. *Desiree would be pretty if she smiled.*

But she couldn't – not even in her eyes.

Rasheed exalted his box, and made his way to the exit. He wondered why the unhappiness that roamed stateside lived on streets named after slain Black leaders. And why Black leaders were slain. He wondered about Desiree's life beyond the counter... Who was she past the nametag? And he questioned the possibility of his doughnuts, at the very least, staying warm after the train ride home. *I can always put dem in the microwave.*

Rasheed quickly spun his back against the glass door, both hands on the box, and allowed his weight to usher in the air of the night. *Yeah... Desiree could definitely be hot.* And the streets were defiantly cold. Rasheed thought about trying to revisit the automobile. *Just maybe she would start after a little rest...* But the whisper that promised frustration from disappointment made the public transportation system seem like an easier journey.

At one in the morning, most businesses in the A-Town are slammed shut, windows guarded with metal grates – almost as if the décor is designed to match the buildings whose windows are boarded with plywood and wallpapered with posters that post the next great star on pop culture's horizon. Nonetheless, every few tenements are tagged with very little artistic skill, but a profound statement: *Free Al-Amin.* After all, this was his neighborhood – a place where violence was as Amerikkkan as cherry pie.

The West End Mall, which could barely be classified as a mall, even looked abandoned. That is, of course, other than the row houses of homeless people... Squatters that slept on the padding of newspapers. Rasheed moved with swiftness down the sidewalk. Avoiding the broken glass and the eyes longing for the treasure in his white and green parcel. As Rasheed darted across the street in front of the rail station, he noticed there was no attendant. *That's a bet... I wa'n't trying to pay no dolla' seven'y five no how.* Acting as if he was fumbling through his pockets for a token or rail card or whatever, he waited until he could hear the electricity dancing off the third rail. He then, pulled the bar of the turnstile backwards, slid through the opening, ran up the escalator, and bounced through the doors just as the warning bell ushered their closing. Rasheed took a seat and caressed the box of Krispy Kremes.

*   *   *

I'm riding
               subway, transit, metro lines
MARTA, SEPTA, the L is fine
                                     I'm just
tryna forge my way in this wilderness
I'm feelin this —
world cave in...
                    my skin I blend
wit' seat cushions
I keep lookin' at
the ole man at the end of the aisle
it's as if his eyes are

                                        miles away
from his soul...
a world wit' too many toll booths and
so many Blacks are tokens
stuck into the turnstile
never to return
while the world pushes through

the train shakes on its tracks...

For Rasheed, public transportation was the ultimate Catch 22. On one hand, he was an artist... His mind painting the colors of reality long before his hand touched a brush and his soul stroked the canvas. He had begun to make a real name for himself with his visual masterpieces, and the large bulk of his work was created on bumpy bus rides, razor sharp street corners, and on the fleeing treetops of interstate highways... treetops that knew his name and empathized with his struggle, thanks to the frequency of their interactions. On the other hand, it was also these places that whispered to Rasheed of his ever-approaching demise. A demise that was void of earthly accomplishments. And the public transportation system seemed as if it were the crown harbor for such a reminder. It was filled with the pains of no purpose – a pain that Rasheed would rather forget than to have to truly acknowledge, a whisper that Rasheed yearned to escape.

'cause the chatter
is
chip
ping
a
way
at my back
but my eyes cain't escape this
gaze that lacks
life
I try to focus on the fact that

darker days bring light
but I cain't phase out
what happens to souls
that cain't find their way through the haze
and stay lost at sea in the abyss of the night

"What kind... blunt... you need?"

Rasheed stared blankly at the desert colored man behind the scratched up Plexiglas, squeezing the very life out of his box of room temperature donuts. He wondered, as he always did, how these immigrants from far off lands find their way past US customs and into the bowels of every Niggerville, Ghetto Amerikkka to set up shop? His mind whispered thoughts of how they were Arab and Korean and African and every other nationality that Amerikkka had waged war on, yet they were granted a safe passage into impoverished neighborhoods. Briefly, Rasheed's eyes scanned the stock of the variety store (which was suppose to be a gas station, but sold very little gas since most people in the neighborhood relied on public transportation).

But everything else was for sell. Protected by the bulletproof glass and the oversized Arab (or Indian or whatever he was), who constantly fingered the Glock 17 that sat on the counter; the wall of assorted goods was far past the point of clutter. Rasheed's mind took inventory in agitated hisses: there were twenty different brands of condoms (lifestyles, Trojans, magnums, ruff riders, ribbed, lubricated, and ultrasensitive). Rasheed thought of Keisha.

There were playing cards, rolling dice, and gold plated handheld scales to compliment the mini-zip locks that were hidden beneath the counter. The make shift plywood shelves housed a vast array of Robutussin, Advils, Goody's headache powder, and Pepto Bismol. There were boxes of cigars and an overhead bend of cigarettes. And finally, Rasheed focused his attention back to the counter bombarded with an open pack of Doral's (so that single cigarettes could be sold), an assortment of ginseng, some not-so-natural sex enhancement pills, and every individually wrapped cigar that could possible be for sell. His mind snickered at the lack of organization in the one-stop shop, but the amusement seemed to only add further agitation to his already festering thoughts.

"What kind... blunt... huh?"

The impatient tone of the attendant, more commonly whispered to as Desert Nigga, caused the agitation to ripple into a slight wave of aggression. "Wait a fuckin' minute – I'm tryin' to think!" The tone reflected his annoyance while, at the same time, making Rasheed feel a sense of authority. *Shit, you work for me, Desert Nigga,* spewing in a dirty whisper...a mumble that only his mind could hear.

He waited an extra moment to drive his point to everybody, but mainly to himself. And then, he requested the exact same cigar he always purchased. "Let me get a Garcia in the tube," he snarled, throwing the money into the slot constructed for safe exchanges. The storeowner grabbed the money, rang up the transaction, and placed Rasheed's blunt and change back into the slot. He snatched his blunt and stormed out of the store, leaving his four pennies abandoned – sacrificed for a greater cause. His point was that he didn't want nor need the pennies. He was saying that he was better than those copper portraits of a guy who didn't care about his freedom either... better than the jungle of merchandise that Arabs and Koreans peddled in his neighborhoods. The storeowner, unfortunately, did not get the point. He did, however, understand that he was now four pennies closer to the dollars that it would take to leave this country of idiots, who lacked the ability to understand the value of small things.

Walking down MLK Rasheed's conversation with Keshia began to whisper in his head. He cringed at the idea of explaining the lack of financial success from his recent road trip. His eyes began to glaze as he thought of having to go without acknowledging the many people who came to view his work – their endless praises. How their eyes shook in astonishment as his art made their souls inevitably recognize their emotions. He didn't want to act as if he didn't adore their presence simply because their pockets did not allow them the luxury of compensating the artist that gave their spirits such a rare gift. As Rasheed's attention started to draw towards the whisper, his walk began to slow, making each step more painful. He thought about Keshia's car not starting and how she let him use it despite the fact that he had no money or a valid driver's license, for that matter.

For a brief second the spray painted tomb distracted the whispers. It read: R.I.P. Rico. He wondered was Rico really resting in peace or was the afterlife just as dubious as the one he was forced to live in right now. The thoughts in Rasheed's head became antagonizing whimpers and irate hisses. He began to curse his talent. And he hated the package in his hand and the one in his pocket and the people who loved his work, and encouraged him to fight the odds that were stacked against him. He hated Keisha for saying she loved him for his passion because it caused him to work harder and want more. But his life seemed to be plagued with roadblocks. He hated the Desert Nigga who took his four pennies… and Desiree for not being able to smile. The public transportation system for transporting slaves….

And then, he turned the key into the lock of the apartment where his name did not appear on the lease. Keshia smiled, "I've been waiting on you all night… I didn't hear that raggedy truck pull in."

"Yeah… it broke down over there on Ralph David."

"Ooohhh… you got donuts," Keshia stood up and playfully snatched the box out of Rasheed's hand, without any acknowledgment of his previous statement, and kissed him with tender depth on his lips. "I missed you," she whispered. "I hate it when you leave," another semi-opened mouth peck landing on his cheek. "But I love to see you return."

Rasheed paused. He saw the truth in Keshia's eyes and his innards shook from the shock of such a loud scream… a scream so honest and so audible that even as the lies of the whisper hissed— Rasheed had already traveled too far out of its reach.

Good Man
by Jon Goode

She just wanted me to be
A Good Man
And Good Lord I wish I could be
What she wants me to be
But the corners been offering me
The ghetto's horn of plenty
And the streets been calling me
24-7, 365, 10-10-220
Women and Men
Play lotto like rummy
Buy dime sacks of my sin
And the money
Helps me bring home the bacon
In this land of milk and honey
But lately
I've been feeling like Michael's older brother Sonny
Drivin' slowly toward that toll booth
I swore to tell her the truth
Nothing but the whole truth.
In a conversation between she and Me
I told her truthfully
I never wanted to be
The one with a semi
Sittin' closely
Against my hand like Isotoners
Some cat trying to give me a Corona
But I've got Remi and bologna
Some Henny, serving rocks like good plenty on the corner
Trying to get close to Good Times
Like Penny and Willona
In this life I gotta take what I need
Because they only
Gonna give me what they want ta'
But please don't give me your sympathy
Que Sera Sera, I'm gonna be what I'm meant to be
Love, I hope you see
I'm trying to hear what you got to say
Like James Did Florida
I'm trying to steal you away

Like Bush did Florida
I'm trying to find a way
Like Juan Ponce De Leon
Did down in Florida
A prince of the streets
Holds signs of the times
That read I've been Adorin ya
But it's four in the morning
The blocks still jumping
And the streets are never yawning
And it seems to me
that these fiends seem to be
Hanging on the crack house like an awning
Some one's got to appease
Their need for crack, X and Speed
And I guess it's gonna be me
And when I get home
Your eyes always softly plead
Always softly asking me please
Baby just try for me
To be a good man
And God knows
For once
I wish I could give her what she wants
But the corners been offering me
The ghetto's horn of plenty
And the streets been calling me
24-7, 365, 10-10-220

"The greatest obstacle to love is fear. It has been the source of all defects in human behavior throughout the ages."

— Mahmoud Mohammed Taha, Sudanese reformer

No Lying in the Dark

Kim Caldwell

That morning, like all mornings, she had risen with the sun. That morning, like all mornings, she went into the kitchen to start breakfast. That morning, like all mornings, she kissed him awake. Like all mornings, she sat across the kitchen table from him and made small talk. Like all mornings, she showered and dressed in her business casual best. Like all mornings, she got into her yuppie BMW. Like all mornings, she listened to the drone of Atlanta's V-103 drones as she manipulated mid-morning traffic on her way to work. Like all mornings, she mourned the losses he would never know because she could never tell him. Like all mornings, she fought demons known and unknown. Like all mornings, her truths hovered above her heart, waiting to get in.

That morning, like all mornings, he rolled into the warmth of her now empty side of the bed. That morning, like all mornings, he listened to the sounds of her rummaging through the cabinets of the kitchen. That morning, like all mornings, he feigned asleep when her lips pressed against his forehead. Like all mornings, he lay silently for stolen moments before joining her at the kitchen table. Like all mornings, he exchanged small talk. Like all mornings, he showered in the guest bathroom. Like all mornings, he adjourned to his side of the double vanity as he prepared for work. Like all mornings, he gave her the obligatory peck on the cheek on his way out of the door. Like all mornings, he drove his car to the Park-N-Ride at the Marta station. Like all mornings, he boarded the train that would transition him from the suburbs to the inner city. Like all mornings, he sunk into his seat with the weight of reality on his shoulders, heart, and mind.

Like all days, both went through the motions, methodically covering their discontentment with masks of misconception. Individually, they knew the lies they were living. Collectively, they committed themselves to those lies. They had stacked one on top of the other until there existed a wall between them and a fortress separating them from the truth.

*   *   *   *   *   *   *   *   *

As she trudged through traffic on her way home, she tuned in to Atlanta's Big Station, V-103. She went and stopped and went and stopped and went and stopped. The motion, or lack thereof, played somewhere on the border of her consciousness because she was lost in the thoughts of the past two years- lost in the memories of missing minutes that she would never be able to recoup. She was lost in the smell of babies she would never be able to touch. She was lost in the feel of cold steel spreading her lips to invade her cervix. She was lost in the sound of quiet suctioning of motherhood membrane and barely formed bones from her uterus. She was lost in the lies that disguised the truth so that he could not recognize it when it stood before him. How could she explain? What words would she use to explain that she had aborted their babies? She had yet to figure out which nouns to place next to what verbs in order to begin. What adjectives would she use to properly qualify her actions? What punctuation would she place at the end of the sentence, "*I aborted our babies*", to legitimize her actions. It was not enough to simply say, "*I didn't want to be a mother.*" She would have to explain that she couldn't be a mother- especially one like her own. She would have to put her childhood under the microscope and display all of the cracks in her foundation. She would have to point out all of the now-faded scars that were still open wounds. She would have to repeat all of the *fat bitches, lazy heifers, and you ain't gonna be shits* that were circulating in her subconscious. How could she ever find comfort in motherhood when she had never found comfort in her own mother? But what language could she use to verbalize the fear that had forced her to make the appointments- the fear that forced her eyes shut in an attempt to force out the faces of her slain babies. How could she say it?

He boarded the train as he headed home. His eyes were focused on the window, watching the passersby pass by. He wondered if they could read the secret behind his eyes. Were they even looking into his eyes? Did anyone ever really look him in the eyes? As the train lurched forward, he refused to relinquish his grip on these people waiting and walking and talking and resting. He hoped that someone would stop the train that would stop his ride into the life that didn't fit- that had never fit. He had forced it on out of fear of his fate. He had forced himself to fit into this fantasy life of wife, home and job- home, wife, and job- job, home, and wife. He had hoped that a child would come soon. He thought that a child would make his life more real. He thought that a child would be an equal exchange for the life he had given up. A child would replace his desire to prowl Piedmont Park after dark in search of a strange man hands to touch him in familiar places. A child would replace the feel of man mouth massaging his member and working up his frenzy only to empty it into the darkness. A child would save him from the empty faces that followed the question, "*Looking for trade?*" A child would slap the "*yes*" from his lips. A child would stand between him and another random bent over lover. A child would take the condom from his hands and replace it with small fingers, leading him from his hidden life. But the child never came. Even after he forced himself hard by turning her over and closing his eyes as he entered her, making it easier to picture a "him" in her place. Several times a month, he rode "him" into her and prayed that one seed would take root because it was a child that would save him.

*   *   *   *   *   *   *   *   *

The car in front of her came to a screeching halt, jolting her from her thoughts. She looked up just in time to prevent a rear-end collision. She had been oblivious in traffic's flow, but now realized that, although she was only a few blocks from home, traffic was at a standstill. Was there an accident up ahead? She turned up the volume on the radio in hopes of finding clarity in a newsbreak. What she discovered was that the entire state of Georgia was blacked out. There were no details to indicate why. The investigation was still in process. She turned off on a side street, took a couple of back roads, and was home in a matter of minutes.

In perfect unison, the train stopped suddenly and the lights went out, causing all bodies on board to bolt forward, including his. Voices invaded the darkness, *"What's going on?" "I'm claustrophobic." "I need to hurry up and get home."* For approximately ten minutes, they sat in complete darkness, trapped by their individual fears that found freedom in the darkness. Men, who would never openly display fear, were desperately stating, *"I'm scared."* Soon the news found its way to their compartment. Georgia was in the middle of a blackout. Everyone on the train began to panic, knowing that the train would not move anytime soon. There was desperation to escape. But, because he was only a few yards away from his stop, he was allowed to walk. He calmly made his way to the next stop, to his car in the Park-n-Ride, and finally, home.

By the time he made it to the door, the sun was setting, streaking the sky in shades of red, purple, and orange. He stood on the doorstep gazing out at the sky, longing for the freedom of color in his world. But they had built this half-muted life that lent itself to this new well of desire to be free of the discontentment- free of the complacent captivity. He walked through the door and immediately felt trapped. Although it was not yet completely dark outside, the warmth of light had been replaced by dank shadows. He found her wandering around the house, strategically placing candles so that there would be no lack of light when darkness finally closed in on them. He pulled her into his arms and planted a kiss on her neck. Involuntarily, she stiffened. She had been so consumed with her own thoughts that she couldn't even pretend to accept his affections. He, also consumed with his own thoughts, didn't notice her flinching away from him. He was too busy pushing back the mental picture of strong hands massaging away the pressures of this life.

"How was your day?"

"Fine, yours?"

"Fine."

"What's for dinner?"

"Sandwiches… not much choice without electricity."

"Mind if I shower first?"

"No… that would be my preference. I can't stand the smell of that train on you."

He went into their bedroom to shower this time. As the hot, steamy water ran down his back, his mind traveled back to the day's thoughts. He wanted so badly to be free of this demon that had altered his desire for women and turned him toward men. He sickened himself every time a man stirred something in him. How could he be a man when he desired men? His mind overflowed with solutions to his problem. Each time, he ended in the same place - only a child would save him. But where was his savior? Because it was such a task to engage in sexual acts with her, he made sure that he only initiated sex when she was ovulating. He knew her schedule. So where was his savior? He had even noticed changes in her body a couple of times. So where was his savior? He had recommended fertility specialists, which she always declined saying, *"When it's time, it will happen."* Where was his savior? He didn't have much more time left. If his savior didn't come soon, he would die. Or succumb to his desires - a tantamount to death.

As darkness settled in, she wandered from room to room with her candle and found herself in what would have been the children's room. Right now, it was substituting as a second guest bedroom - as if they ever had company. She sat the candle on the dresser, and with her mind's eye, began to paint picture perfect. She replaced the queen-sized bed with a convertible crib. The walls became a mural of a meadow drenched in muted pastels. A changing table took form in the corner, while scents of baby lotion, oil, and shampoo filtered through her nostrils and attacked her heart, forcing her into a crumpled ball on the floor. She rocked back and forth, humming a lullaby from her very distant childhood - one that her mother never soothed her with, but she still found comfort in. *Hush little baby… don't say a word. Mama's gonna…* The tears finally flowed. She cried for her murdered babies and their murderer. She assumed the fetal position and cried herself into a silent frenzy until she felt him collecting her into his arms. She had not heard him enter the room. He had just finished his shower and was on his way to the kitchen when he heard her soft moans. He had stood in the doorway watching the truth wash over her. He picked her up, balanced her against his chest and walked over to the bed. He sat down and held her on his lap. He attempted to force her head up so that he could look into her eyes. He wanted to read her pain, but she refused to give him her eyes. He whispered over and over again, *"Baby, what's wrong?"* She shook her head with enough force to rip the dead babies from her mind. She curled up tighter in his lap and wrung her hands in an effort to wipe the blood from her fingers. She was guilty of murder and she could no longer wrap her mind around it. It no longer fit inside of her. It had outgrown her. The words spilled over into the darkness and loomed over them like the shadows that danced around the walls. *"I killed our babies. I murdered our babies."*

He could barely make out her statement...it came out in such a hushed whisper. And with that, her crying lost its silence and she wailed loudly and uncontrollably, inconsolably. He sat there holding her, but really holding himself, using her as a shield to keep his fears at bay. At that moment, she was his safeguard. She was the boundary between him and the thoughts of men lurking in the shadows. They were waiting for him and he knew it. They were waiting for him to display his weakness for wide shoulders and chiseled chins - for the love of a man. At that moment, she was his savior. The crescendo of his cries started on the inside and continued until his entire body shook with the intensity of their reality. He was no longer holding her; she was holding him. His truths were forcing their way in and he knew no one could save him. She was searching for words to comfort him but all she found was a trail of *"I'm sorry's"* that lead back to being sorry. *"I'm so sorry... I know you wanted children but I..."* *"But you what..."* he managed between his sobs. *"I...I..."* she stammered over her explanation of why she could not be a mother. *"YOU WHAT???!"* he roared back at her so suddenly, the force catapulted her from his lap. He stood and frantically scoured the room with his now-red eyes trying to make out the shadows of men attacking him from the corners of his mind. They were approaching with lips ready to kiss, with hands ready to touch, with erect penises ready to prod. There was no child to save him. There was only her. And him. And the truth...

He turned his back to walk out of the door. She managed to get it out just as he made it to the threshold, *"I just don't want to be a mother. I don't know how to be a mother."* He ran from the words or the tempting men lurking in the corners of his savior's bedroom. He went into the kitchen. She found him there with his head buried in his hands. She sat down across from him and reached for his hands. He withdrew. He threw the words across the table like a fast curve ball and they hit her in her ears. They were not angry words or hurt words. They were neither mild nor meek. They just were... a statement of fact no longer sheltered by his fear of demolishing their false foundation. He felt free of the façade. He removed his mask, freed his mouth, and said, *"I don't love you. I have spent the past two years denying myself in hopes that you would never have to know that I'm attracted to men. I have spent two years mastur-bating to memories in the shower. I have been praying and praying for the distraction of a child. Our child. The one that you aborted without even dis-cussing it with me. You stole my chance at freedom..."*

His words sent her reeling. She stood up and started to walk out, but something held her there. She sat back down and reached for his hands again. He withdrew. She reached over and raised his head until she was looking him squarely in the eyes. She read the secret be-hind his eyes and, with hers, begged him to let truth wash over him and her. There they sat across the candlelit table from each other, staring through the flames into each other's eyes. Truth was dancing on the walls.

*   *   *   *   *   *   *   *   *

She awoke to the sun breaking through a sliver in the curtains. She looked up at the clock blinking *12:00*. That morning like all morn-ings, she rose with the sun. That morning like all mornings, he rolled into the warmth of her now empty side of the bed.

Staring

Jon Goode

How the power outage had managed to affect his cell phone he didn't know. All he knew was that he was getting no service. The entire city had been plummeted into darkness as if God himself had said "Let there be no light." A city that never slept had been knocked unconscious. People filed out of their office buildings and shops into the streets where they milled about cluelessly and with what seemed to be more instinct than choice they pulled out their cell phones. They pulled out their phones in an effort to call the world and appraise them of these dark times. In a city filled with millions of people they all felt suddenly utterly alone. Misery loves company and to that end they all began trying to dial.

He stared at his phone and occasionally glanced up and around to see if anyone else was sharing his experience. His experience being one of total cellular betrayal, not on the basic building block of life level but on the basic plan by Sterizon level. The expression on his face was like that of a child who'd just discovered that the whole Santa Clause thing is a hoax. The people around him stared at their cell phones in disbelief also as if to say "Et Tu Brute?" The street was filled with blank expressions staring at little hand held blank screens waiting for some glimmer of hope. Hoping against hope that the signal bars would stair step from the nothingness of zero to the magical all powerful five bars

Bars? Oddly enough bars seemed to be a re-occurring theme in his life. As a child he loved to play on the monkey *bars* swinging and swaying on the steel beams until his arms shook uncontrollably from fatigue and the flesh at the base of his fingers, just where his skinny digits met his chubby hands, would blister. He endured so much pain for so much pleasure. As a pre teen his mother had insisted that he take up an instrument so his jungle gym prowling and monkey bars expertise had been replaced with the mastery of classical scales and *bars*. His music teacher was a relentless task master that would crack him across the hands with a ruler whenever he made the slightest error. Through time, and ironically classical conditioning, his play became beautiful and flawless and he found himself enjoying the music he'd learned to create at the request of his mother and the behest of a ruler. He endured so much pain for so much pleasure. In his teen age years he grew rebellious and fell in with a wild crowd. His new found friends picked him up one day after school in a car that unbeknownst to him was stolen. None of them were of a driving age so when a car filled with fourteen year old boys that only looked twelve years old drove past an officer's squad car the officer easily assessed the situation and took them into custody. The boys were all put in a lock up to scare them until their parents arrived. He stood there drenched in his adolescent fear, his hands gripping the steel *bars*. He thought back to the jungle gym and the feel of the bars in his hand as he swung. He thought back to music class and the feel of the instrument as he manipulated the chords and played the bars. Then he looked at the bars before him now and knew that this was not the way. He'd enjoyed the joy ride with his friends but the cost was too high. He'd endured too much pain for too little pleasure. He was scared straight from that point on and fell in with a new crowd of friends that helped him on his fast track to college. His college years had been spent in and out of class and in and out of *bars* picking up women and reviling in song. His post undergraduate and post law school years had been spent trying to pass the *bar* exam. Today however, he found himself staring at his cell phone hoping the intense glare of his eyes would scare five bars into the upper left hand corner of the screen. His gaze must not have been that intimidating.

He wanted to call his wife and make sure she was alright. He knew she was not a mousy woman and that she could take care of herself but calling her seemed like the right thing to do. He'd met her in one of those college bars and within a week he'd found out that she knew her away around the bar, around the dance floor, around the kitchen and around the bedroom. How could he not marry her? Their whirlwind romance ended with him staring down from an altar, up an aisle flanked by family and friends as her father dropped her off next to him, like a UPS express package, and told him to sign for her and take her home. He promptly did both and they began to play married.

The secret unbeknownst to even them was that through all their college years of lust making, drunken revelry, club hopping and occasional class attendance they never really got to know each other. She was a nice enough girl it seemed and he a descent fellow and they got along well enough and they dated for a couple of uninterrupted years so the next logical step seemed to be marriage. So they followed the path that seemed so clear at the time. Their first night alone in their apartment as newlyweds let them in on their own secret. The evening was marked with an incredibly awkward silence at the dinner table. Neither knew what to say to the other. Neither really knew the other. He turned on the television that night in an effort to break the awkward silence and they never ate dinner without it again.

"Make still the Ferry can we do!" A man screams and pulls him from his thoughts. The man appears to be one of the cities many transients. He stares at the man as he continues to speak in a language that he recognizes as English but the words seem to be coming together in a way that defies comprehension. The city is a melting pot of races, creeds, colors and dialects and the sonic gumbo spewing from this mans mouth is a vocal mutt.

"What are you saying?" he asks "Slow down."

"The Ferry?! If hurry we make the Ferry still across the river do can. The killed power subway cars stopped?"

He stares at this man who he's sure he's never seen before in his life as he lets his mind try to construct a discernable sentence from the word fragments thrown at him like a dictionary grenade. He finally pieces it all together.

"Oh the Ferry? No, I live in the city but you better hurry if you plan on making the ferry."

The man then puts out his hand and speaks in perfect English through less than perfect teeth.

"I see...Spare some change then?"

What a hustle. The good Samaritan hustle is a classic. He drops a couple of coins in the transient mans hands thinking what can it hurt. The little it cost him could mean a lot to this guy. The man mumbles something inaudible as they move off in opposite directions. He looks over his shoulder and sees the guy giving the same gibberish spill to someone else. The power may have failed but the street hustle is self powering, self serving and always on.

He looks skyward and notices he has a couple of hours of day light left so he starts his trek home. Somewhere in the back of his mind in the dark recesses of his sub conscious he can feel a certain apprehension about heading home growing. It's almost as if the darkness is feeding this feeling. As the darkness grows nearer the feeling begins growing stronger. He doesn't want to acknowledge it but he can't ignore it. What are he and his wife going to do when he gets home? The TV had been their saving grace their three years of marriage was totally supported by the television. They didn't usually talk unless it was about something on TV, most times it seemed like they turned on the TV to avoid having to talk at all. She had "Sex and the City," and he had "The Satellite Sports package," which afforded him the opportunity to watch every game, of every sport, in the free world and as an added bonus it allowed him to ignore her utterly. Even when they went to bed they set the sleep timer for one hour and let the TV glow, hum and murmur them a lullaby. In restaurants they sat near the ever present TV and either looked at their plates or looked at the screen, but never each other. He was slowly beginning to realize that in all actuality he didn't even know this woman. He'd met a stranger in a bar one night, slept with that stranger, married that stranger and now he was walking home through the twilight to that stranger. This realization gave the night a darkness far greater than that of the blackout.

He'd never seen so many people out in the streets before, which seemed impossible because this was a busy city. But people were everywhere, hustling their way toward the ferry or walking across the bridges, all in an effort to hurry home to their loved ones, one would suspect. A few people accepted the futility of it all and just sat around waiting for everything and everyone to calm down. A few guys even struck up games of hand ball to kill the time. He however continued walking, taking it all in as he strolled. He looked at the nervous Bodega owners; they seemed to be keeping one eye on the sky and one eye on the street. They could feel a night of looting and rioting quickly approaching. That didn't stop them from exploiting the situation at hand however, as they sold bottled water and batteries at "I know you've got to have it" prices, taking full advantage of the tragedy. He watched as the Police Officers began to take posts on the street corners, letting there presence be known. They were there to discourage any raucous behavior. Even with the added blanket of protection the shop owners still looked incredibly nervous. They knew that if people really wanted what they had in their stores a couple of cops wouldn't stop them. If they *really* wanted it, an entire army couldn't stop them.

The sun continued its dance across the sky playing hide and seek with the horizon. The orange and purple sunset unmarred by the man made urban luminescence was absolutely breathtaking. He himself was at a loss for breath, but it had nothing to do with the setting of the sun, it was due to his own lack of regular cardiovascular exercise. As he walked he loosened his tie and unfastened the top button of his shirt. He could feel the sweat beginning to trickle down his back. It had been a hot day and promised to be an extremely warm and humid evening. From nowhere a breeze caught him full in the face and reminded him of the simple pleasures of life. He began to wonder why he and his wife had never taken advantage of the night air. He wondered why they'd never just strolled hand in hand and stared at the night sky or even more simply stared into each others eyes. He wondered if she even liked to take strolls. In his mind he was relatively sure her eyes were brown, but he felt like he was guessing. He realized there was so much he didn't know about her. What were her wants, her desires, her dreams, he had not a clue. What did she do for fun and leisure? What was she passionate about? Who was this woman?

The sun had totally set as he rounded the corner and moved toward their apartment. People littered the steps of the building listening to battery powered radios and talking to one another. People who he was sure had never passed a word between them found common ground, common experience and conversation in the shared events of the blackout. He spoke and nodded to his newly found neighbors as he made his way to the door of the building. He met each of their stares and greeted them with a smile that was warmly returned.

"Elevators out," a voice stated as both a courtesy and a warning.

"Thank you," he replied over his shoulder as he steadied his mind to climb the four flights of steps that lay in wait. He had to fight to steady the voice in his head that began shouting "What are you and she going to talk about? You don't even know this woman!! FOR ALL YOU KNOW YOU MIGHT NOT EVEN LIKE THIS WOMAN YOU LOVE!!!" He took a deep breath of the stale stairwell air and found solace in the rhythm of his own breathing. He began thinking that maybe she realized that she didn't know him either and turned in early. Maybe she was already sleep and they could circumnavigate this event. Tomorrow the television would be back on and they could continue to play married.

By the time he reached the top of the fourth flight of steps his legs were burning and aching with pain. He'd sweated through his shirt and discarded his tie three blocks back somewhere. He fumbled with his keys, partly due to the darkness, and partly trying to stall. He found the key, found the lock, found the nerve and pushed the door open.

The first things he noticed were the candles everywhere. The soft candles light was casting flickering shadows against the walls, it was absolutely entrancing. Sitting in the middle of the floor was a blanket with two pillows sitting opposite each other. Between the pillows were two plates and more candles. The plates, adorned with what looked to be peanut butter and jelly sandwiches and potato chips, were flanked by a pitcher of red Kool-Aid. She stood in the hallway just beyond the indoor picnic scene. She had on a pair of his boxers and a tank top. She smiled at him with a warmth and sincerity that almost brought tears to his eyes. "Why had this stranger done this for a man she didn't even know," he thought to himself.

"This is the best I could do with no power and short notice," she said as she crossed the room, hugged and kissed him. A kiss laced with passion as her breasts met his chest and her hips sought out his. He never would have imagined that she housed such passion and romance...he never would have thought.

At just that moment their apartment lights began to flash and flicker as power began to be restored to some areas of the city. A white dot appeared at the center of the television. The dot began to grow and the televisions volume grew with it. The dot took shape and form and became a picture. Her eyes went from the television, to the ceiling lights, to his eyes. Her heart, her shoulders and her smile sank. She picked up the remote control, turned to the game and began to blow out the candles.

And just as suddenly as the television and lights had come on, they went out again. She could still see the glow coming in through the windows from the street lights and she could hear the neighbors stereo playing. She turned to find him standing by the light switch, the televisions power cord pulled from the wall socket and dangling in his hand. The cities blackout was ending but it seemed that theirs was beginning anew. There in the darkness away from the distractions of the world he was being introduced for the first time to his wife of three years. He sat on his pillow by his peanut butter and jelly sandwich. She re-lit the candles she'd extinguished and took the seat opposite him.

"I was wondering," he began, still feeling the dull ache in his legs "If you'd like to take a walk with me tonight and just...talk." She smiled, as her black eyes stared into the brown eyes of this man that she was sure... she'd never met before.

just enough
by Kim Caldwell

i criticize his poetry between licks
and i compliment him on how the stroke of his pen
permeates power
i languish late nights
on the tip of his tongue
and he whispers my tune tone deaf
but i sing anyway
humming the sound track
to the movie sifting through his mind
and i pray
that tomorrow is as good as today
and i pray
that our yesterdays are truly behind us
and i pray
that our fears follow the hollowed halls
of what used to be
never distorting the lens that captures us
picture perfect
feeding and fucking
laughing and touching
smoking and loving
crying
and
holding
and
freeing
and
fighting
and
learning
and
living
and
being
and
growing
and
growing
and

growing
and sometimes he opens his chest just enough
so i can see his heart
and sometimes i open my eyes just enough
so he can see my soul
and sometimes i open
just wide enough
and he pushes just deep enough
to make us whole
and sometimes we're one
and sometimes we're two
singles hanging out
two lovers loving
just loving
and sometimes we're friends
and sometimes we're not
and sometimes i miss him
and sometimes i don't
and sometimes i
never i
always i love him
and always i trust him
and always
and always
and always
i believe in him just enough
to dangle right on the edge of the world
because he loves me just enough
not to let me fall
there was something in me
that called out to him
or something in him
that called out to me
or something in us
that called out to we
the technicalities are mere distractions
because we met right in the center of
what's supposed to be
and what may be today
may leave us tomorrow
and i love him just enough
to be content with today
and he loves me just enough
not to promise tomorrow
and sometimes we argue

and sometimes we smile
and sometimes we kiss
and sometimes we frown
and sometimes we fuck
and sometimes we
never we
always we make love
through our movements
that mimic our motives
because he loves me just enough
to mean what he says
and i love him just enough
to do what i mean
and we love each other just enough
to love each other
just enough

"Throughout history it has been the inaction of those who could have acted, the indifference of who should have known better, the silence of justice when it mattered most, that has made it possible for evil to triumph."

— Haile Salassie, emperor of Ethiopia

" UNTITLED #7"
by Malik Salaam

let me

make my mark

so I – – may be remembered

as a member of mankind

that managed to maneuver

past some of this madness

and lived on further than/ the moment

let me

make my mark

so that those still living

will long to hear my legacy

as my life is sung in lullabies

and love songs – –

and played by seasoned thespians

in

low budget films...

so that the colors of my life

may not dim

to the death of

black and white

I write tags on subway walls

and wreck shop wit' rhymes

that I rehearse in public places

in hopes that I will elude

the famous photo line-up

instead my face will be plastered to billboards

and in honor of my burial

flowers will be burned

and beautiful sisters will unlatch their bra straps

to decorate my tombstone

and honor me

with their first born carrying my namesake

let me

make my mark

so that I will not be forgotten

and my folks

will do more than tattoo my

nickname on their neckline/ fore they too must die

let me

make my mark

so that my memory

stirs the souls of vandals

and warriors that the world

has dismissed as vagrants — so

as I was done

> *let me*

make my mark

so that where I have fell short

others may continue in my cause

and the many colors of my life

will not suffer

the death of / black and white.....

my mark

Picture Perfect

Yaminah Ahmad

"You are so beautiful," I whispered. I just stood there…at first, glancing. But then, it was so beautiful – I couldn't tear my eyes away. The more I stared, the more my eyes became fixated on the intricate details, the details no one cared about or even bothered to investigate. Most people don't study beauty because we have this universal consensus on what beauty is and what it isn't. We prefer the concepts…like babies. They say a baby is beautiful because it's polite – and they're cute and cuddly and they smell good… And all of that is true; but for me, that's not why a baby is beautiful. A baby is beautiful because they are the purest reflection of God. Babies love unconditionally and without judgment. And you can love a baby back, without worrying if, one day, this love will be depleted. Its river forever runs deep. Babies embody infinite possibilities and their very existence makes you hopeful that somehow, your life will change and change for the better. And for me, when I stare at this…this work of art, it makes me a believer.

"Look, they made a mistake. See, the outline is crooked," a woman says to her friend with a smidgen of pride about her discovery. I turn my head and watch her as she walks off. Her stride is one of confidence, probably from her ego boost. I don't usually go around making quick assumptions about people; but I think, somehow, she feels better about herself because she was able to identify, what she believes to be, a flaw. And now that this mistake, this error, is exposed for what it truly is, she can feel some sort of security knowing that she isn't the only flawed creation existing in this world. I assume she feels comforted by that. I take a step closer to see for myself. I see the crooked outline. I also see two distinct colors overlapping in an awkward area. I see several identical images shaped differently and I see unutilized space. I see all those things. Yet, when I look at it in its entirety, I see how all of it creates the beauty. I smile and take another step forward, wanting to touch it. I want to connect to this…this creation that has me so transfixed. As I reach out my hand, I notice a scar. I place the wound to my heart and begin rubbing it with my index finger.

My memory is tricky. I can't recall a particular moment in time through names and dates, or even a description of where I was and what I was doing. But if you describe to me how I felt: happy, sad, depressed or giddy, then I will remember. Once I identify the proper emotion, I can tell you what I wore, who was there, the stupid conversations and what we ate. I need to know how I felt before I can recreate the scene in my head. It can be a long process, but like I said, it's tricky. Sometimes, though, I can see something, like my favorite skirt, and remember the last time I wore it and my mind is flooded with all kind of images. Yet, it really doesn't have any significance until I remember the feeling of that night. *Did my skirt and I have a good time?* It's my favorite skirt, which accentuates my butt and makes my legs look longer. So I know I had a good time because I was feeling good. After all, long after that moment disappears into the abyss of my memory, I find that the feeling never dies. And when I look down at the scar that is, once again, finding comfort nestled between my breasts, I remember how I felt when I got it.

When I look at this scar, I remember a time when I was dying. I remember dying a slow and painful death...and then, being reborn. The pain was so severe and yet, physically undetectable. I would rub my hands over my head, my chest and stomach, hoping that one of my body parts would ache. Then, I could go to a doctor (although I had no health insurance), identify the source of my pain, get some drugs and go on living out my monotonous existence. But deep in my heart I knew what ailed me. I knew the minute I sat down at my cubicle. It started when I breathed the air. As I touched the keyboard and exchanged morning pleasantries, the stench of burning dreams and abandoned hope, with its gaseous remains, formed a thick translucent cloud over my desk. Each day, I would look at this cloud, this deathbed, which lay to rest many who have come and gone in this chair. I would inhale the nauseating stink of its remains, and vomit a miniscule piece of myself that would immediately disappear into the cloud. This was my morning ritual – four years of working 10-hour days for five days a week. I was feeling a heavy weight upon my heart. I realized this massive load was applying pressure to an almost empty chamber, which once held the very core of who I was. The more I gagged, the more the cloud had an eerie familiarity. The contents of that chamber were slowly dissipating. The laws of physics told me that eventually, something was going to break. Looking at the cloud living above my head, I knew it was going to be my spirit. And since the body cannot live without the spirit, I feared for my life...I was dying.

So each day I would sit there – typing and smiling, typing and smiling, typing and smiling, knowing that at any given moment, I could collapse and die of sheer misery. Even with this thought festering inside my mind, I continued to work as if nothing was wrong. I felt like I had no choice – too many responsibilities demanded that I forgo my happiness and succumb to the humdrum that so many people accept and label as "living." So I would make myself feel better by luxuriating in ability to (barely) pay my bills. "After all," I told myself, "it could be worse. I could be unemployed and living on the streets..." The internal chastising always worked. It snapped me back into what I thought was reality, but really was stagnation.

One day at work, I was called into a meeting in which I was told my performance was satisfactory. I'm thinking, "Cool, give me my money!" But then, there was a long drawn out explanation, peppered with corporate jargon about downsizing and how my satisfactory performance saved me from being laid off. I was told that, although there wasn't enough money to give me a raise, I proved myself worthy of additional responsibilities. Oh, and my loyalty to the company was also appreciated. To say I was livid is an understatement. It doesn't describe the burning pit down in my stomach. My insides became a volcano. With each breath, I exhaled smoky halos, as if a cigarette lay between my lips. I needed a 'cigarette break' to cool off, so I started walking with no destination in mind. I just wanted to feel the breeze on my face and, somehow, remember a moment in time when I was happy. I found myself standing in front of my car and a crazy thought flew in and out of my mind. I was standing there with my purse because I always carried it with me whenever I left the office, even for a break. I turned back to look at the office door and then stared at my car. I started fumbling through my purse and found my keys. I opened the door and sat halfway in the seat with my feet still touching the ground. My hands began rubbing the steering wheel as if it needed consoling – like it knew what I was thinking and wanted me to consider its feelings. *Who's going to pay for me? We still need to get that knocking noise checked out. Don't do it!* I heard myself snicker out loud. My mind was having a conversation with itself and I felt like I was eavesdropping. Not only was I dying, but I was also going crazy in the midst of it. I thought it was crazy to quit a job without another one lined up. So, I settled on the idea of job-hunting in between working, hoping this would prolong my life just a little bit more and give me time to save up some money. I nodded my head in agreement with all parties involved and started locking up the car. As I turned to walk away, I realized my skirt was caught in the door. I started tugging on it with both hands, thinking it would just slip out. After a couple pulls, I heard it rip inside the door. I got my key out, opened the door and saw my favorite skirt with a highly visible tear. A small nail was peeking its head through the door and still had the seams within its grasp. I got frustrated and started untangling it. My 'cigarette break' was over and I knew someone would be looking for me. I continued to yank the skirt until I felt a sharp pain on my hand. I looked down and saw a small gash leaking the rest of my vitality from my body. I cradled my hand in my chest and started whimpering.

There was enough blood to cover my hand and my shirt was now stained. From a distance, it probably looked as if my heart was actually bleeding and my hand was working to stop the pain. I sat down in my car and stepped on the hanging remains of my skirt to rip off a piece of material. I wrapped it tightly around my hand, which slowed down the blood flow. I was so angry, but not at my car or the nail. I was angry because I knew by the look of the cut I would need stitches and I didn't have any insurance. I looked at the office door and my mind began this twisted conversation with itself.

"That's why you can't leave now. You know they know you deserve a raise. Once they get everything straight, you'll get one. You can't go to another job and start all over. You got too much time invested."

"I don't think I can take another day at this place. It's killing me."

"Look, it's not going to take that long. They know they owe you."

"I can't even afford to go to the doctor."

"You can't afford to leave either. Just stay a little while longer…you got your title, you got your space and they let you slip in late and leave a little bit early too. Besides, you got all that vacation time."

"But I can't afford to go anywhere. I can't remember the last time I actually went somewhere…fun."

"This isn't about fun; this is about being able to pay your bills. Rent is due in one week and your car note in another two weeks. What you gon' do? You can't do nothing else other than stay. Don't worry, it will work out."

For a split second I was able to step outside of myself. And what I saw petrified me. I saw a woman in an abusive relationship that was too scared to leave. There she sat, nursing an injury, knowing that if she goes back, it's a possibility that she might die. She sees her life slipping away and yet, she doesn't see the urgency. Her life is on the line, but she believes, somehow, things will get better. I wondered how bad it has to get before she decides to leave. And then, if she does leave, will she just find herself in another dangerous relationship? When does the cycle end?

That question jolted my spine into a straight line. Even if I got another job, I knew it wouldn't make me happy. In the ten years of working full-time to build my so-called career, I couldn't remember a feeling of bliss. Nothing about what I do excited me… Sure, it impressed my family and friends. I could throw my title in their faces and feel some sort of validation. It was like I mattered because this company said you can call me 'this,' and 'this' means something somewhere to somebody. But in all honesty, beyond the looks of approval, it meant nothing to me. And it bothered me that I spent ten years working at something and can't remember a good feeling. I then settled on trying to remember the last time I smiled and really meant it…nothing. I was too young to be this jaded about life. At that moment, a co-worker spotted me in the parking lot. She walked over to my car and informed me that our supervisor was looking for me and I needed to get back in the office. She didn't even bother to ask about my hand or the stain on my shirt. I knew right then and there that if I fell out and died, nobody would care. I would be replaced like the many souls that came before me. *Why love somebody who don't love you back?* I thought to myself. I started the car and drove off with a huge smile on my face.

I continued to encircle the scar on my hand as I remember that moment in my life. Now, when I meet someone and they notice the scar, I have to go into a spill about 'the incident' and how I didn't have insurance, so it healed looking the way it does. Usually, they tell me to go to a plastic surgeon. But I just laugh at them because I know they don't see the beauty in this birthmark. Every time I look at my hand, I am reminded about how I took a chance on me. And as I look up and stare, again, at the crooked outline and all the other imperfections of this creation, I realized I couldn't fully appreciate it without having my own flaws. I took a couple steps back to absorb the big picture. I nodded my head in gratitude – for true beauty not only can be admired, but it also reveals the beauty of its admirer. And that is something I will never forget.

bamboozled
by Kim Caldwell

they are watching you
waiting
wistfully wishing that you would slip up
and fall
prey to their prayers
to be rid of your young black ass
they push past your pride
and peel down your purpose layer by layer
they expose your black soul
and still manage to call you *nigger*
how dare you smile in spite of your past
how dare you rise in spite of your past
how dare you love and laugh and dance
how dare you manage to still be a man
while they are watching
and the way you love your children
because little loved black babies learn to live
beyond the scope of scathing stares
they are watching the way you listen
to borrowed wisdom of poets and prophets
while ignoring their politics and preachers in pulpits
they contemplate the detriment of free thought
while watching you exercise your intelligence
even they know that educational inequalities
echo into tomorrow
daddy didn't know how to read
so he saw no need in teaching his son
they watched him
blood blending into skin ripped raw
by hate
each lick left reminders that black men can't
can't read
can't write
can't think
but they real easy lynch
they watched you mobilize your movement
toward complete independence
then tapped into your motivation

in attempts to decode your method
and manipulate your message
before it reaches the masses
they are watching you
they assigned your name
rank and serial number
slipped subliminal slices of the american pie
right past your sacredness
while you slumbered
and then placed right you in the line of fire
where they shot you full of bullshit
and then watched you feed it to our kids
they slipped profit right past your promise
promised you the next american idol
top model apprentice
pandering pacifiers
and you purchase a plentiful bounty
of houses
and cars
and platinum
and prada
you date
honies
and hoochies
and actors
and models
and forget that you are being watched
and forget that you have always been watched
and forget that you will be always be watched
so you display behavior unbecoming of the sun
purposely disconnecting your circuitry to the One
and forget that you are not a nigger
no matter how many times you are told you are one
or how many times you are treated like one
or how many time you act like one
you are not a nigger
but they will never know
until you stop portraying yourself as one
honeycutt copies chanting
nigger anthems
sleep-n-eat sideshow freaks
shucking and jiving
to the tune of multi-million dollar contracts
and multi-million dollar paychecks
and multi-million pairs of eyes staring

and judging
and watching
and waiting
for
you
to
slip
up
and
fall

Bells and Silence

Amir Sulaiman

Ding-ding. That bell means money. I know when I hear that bell some-one is coming into my store. I also know that the only reason someone would come into my store is to buy something, and I know when they buy something, I make money. That ding never gets old.

The ding never wears my nerves. Some people play mistress and slave to get their rocks off. Some people like the whole 'pimp and ho' thing. My fantasy, which I play out everyday, is producer and consumer. I'd take a dollar over a dame, any day. I prefer cash to ass, without a doubt. It does it for me. The ding makes my nipples hard. That ding is erotic. I don't care if it's a pretty young thang buying a soda. It could be an old man buying his Newports. It could be some youngster coming to buy those little razors to place under his tongue or to chop his crack rocks. Young, old, male, female, black, or white, it turns me on. Ding me, baby. I sell everything. I'll sell anything. I'm sprung on the ding.

It's been good. All I've been doing is sitting in here listening to my oldies on WAOK, reading my papers and dinging all day. This station said it got up to ninety degrees or something like that today. Even though I sit in the A/C, I know how hot it is. These folks been in here all day buying cold drinks. I paid my rent today just off the O.E. I'm killin' them in the heat; they can't help but to drink when it's hot like this. Especially when they try to quench some thirst with those sodas and beers. They never stop coming! All day ding, ding, ding.

Awwww yeaaah...that DJ is playing that Sam Cook. Woooo!!! Classic.

"It's too hard livin'...but I am afraid to die...don't know what's up there beyond the..."

Naw, naw, naw, this raggedy radio done finally gave out on me. Not on my Sam. Damn.

Reggie is no technician so, he just smacks the radio in some hope that the smacking would cure the radio of its disobedience. It's not that irrational, as he has smacked other things and other people and the smack, indeed, rendered them in line. No such luck with the radio though. It just sits there stubborn, staring and unshaken by his yelling and smacking.

As Reggie sits back to take a time-out and catch his breath, he hears something. Something he has never heard in the store before. He hears silence. Heavy, numbing silence. The silence that he usually avoids at all cost. The silence he washes out with radio and TV and humming and talking, even if only to himself. Just as long as there is no silence. This was the white cloud of silence that makes him hear his own thoughts. Not those thoughts that he's grown accustomed to, but those thoughts he thought he didn't think about anymore. The thoughts about his youthful aspirations crept into his consciousness. There were many aspirations but none of them were selling lotto and liquor to people with no luck and bad livers. The thoughts about his first love and worst fear usually were whispers, but now so loud, his ears could hear them as if his mouth was saying them. But then, he is saved from himself by the ever-soothing DING.

A brown boy rushes into the store, striding with intent. He walks quickly towards the ice cream cooler with a dirty dollar clenched in his hand and the look of anticipation on his face. He slides the glass open and ponders his choices. He settles on an orange Popsicle with the expected "surprise" of vanilla ice cream in the center. He grabs his hard earned treat only for his fist to close upon the stick and the sweet orange and white leak from the paper onto the floor.

"What the hell you doing, boy!"

Reggie rushes from behind the counter to snatch up this brown boy who has defiled his sanctuary. The boy is once shocked by his disappointing treat and second, by this grown man's hands grabbing him by his shoulders.

"I ain't do nothin'. Your stuff ain't even froze. I ain't do it."

Reggie's attention turns towards his freezer. He lets the boy go and the boy wastes no time in making his escape back into the street. Reggie sticks his head into the freezer and he hears 'it' again. The silence. It surrounds him and follows him from cooler to cooler like a reoccurring nightmare. Between the silence, his thoughts, and his warm OE, he thinks he may lose his grip. Like a hot breeze rushing over his brain, he realizes that his beloved store is out of power. He is okay until the trembling starts. It begins in his knees, and travels, at a moderate pace, towards his heart and his toes simultaneously. He turns towards the door and runs out into the street, in a similar manner as the brown boy minutes earlier. In the street he finds everyone that lives on the block. Everyone is outside. Everyone is silent, looking at everyone else. Everyone has their mouths open and their eyes wide, wandering in the street for answers. Everyone is looking deep into everyone else in hope of finding a reason or an instruction or a way not to panic. No one knows. And then, finally... Finally, finally noise. Finally a voice, broadcast from some other place of authority, blares out into the street from the trunk of a midnight Cadillac. Ahhhh... a radio. The silent citizens gather around the young man's trunk like primitives gathering around the village shaman. They hear not what they feared, but rather, they hear what they had never imagined. The whole state is out of power. A wave of audible sorrow vibrates through the crowd.

Reggie turns and turns, as if at one of these turns will find a refuge or a solution... but he is just turning in circles in the middle of the street. He is a whirling dervish without the euphoria. He decides to take cover in his store, his sanctuary, even if it is silent.

He stands on the inside of the Plexiglas staring out. He can see the crowd changing before his eyes. As the sky is turning from blue to red, the crowd is changing from astonished to desperate; then from desperate to frustrated. He hurries to lock his store door as he sees the people whispering and pointing at him. He flips his sign to read: "Sorry Closed," but this does not deter them. They walk past the store, on the sidewalk out front. As they pass, they stare at him with a knowing. They know like he knows that the police will over extend themselves. They know like he knows that all cameras and alarm systems are not functioning. They know, like he knows, that he has food, drink and cash locked in his little sanctuary. They know like he knows that Plexiglas can only do so much. They are just waiting for the darkness and it won't be long now.

Like brown vultures, they slowly circle the block just waiting for the sky to blacken. The light is slipping from the horizon, smoothly sliding from the skyline like a bright, silk sheet being dragged from the city sky. He sees his life receding, like the light, into the darkness of not.

Even as a youth he was never afraid of the dark; but the dark of this night fills his heart with such fear that he has to restrain his hands. His hands, involuntarily and irrationally, want to try to pull the day back from the western horizon or push the blackness back to the east. The comfort of light is the comfort of life; but he must accept the fact that it will get dark.

As the whisper of day sinks out of sight, he grabs his pistol and runs to the storage room and waits. He can taste fear on his tongue. His hand shakes to the degree that he could not load the six bullets into his pistol without having to take deep breaths between each bullet. His head is hot with anxiety. Each pore on his bald spot acts like a microscopic geyser shooting out liquid fear that runs down his face and neck, his chest and back, his thighs and ankles. It is now dark, still and silent. Fear does not whisper in his ear. Fear is a wild banshee screaming at his head - she is screaming silence that could pop his eardrums. His eyes jut around in the dim storage space. His ears try to extend themselves past his head to steal a sound from outside, perhaps a warning of the inevitable. His mind fast-forwards through the possible scenarios. All of them end badly. Very badly. He can only hold himself, rocking back and forth on an overturned orange mopping bucket.

Was that a knock outside or a thought in his head?
KNOCK KNOCK.

They are finally here. The knocks become louder, more rapid and more rabid. He can hear the muffled yells of former customers now wrought insane by heat and silence. The knocking is now banging and yelling, giving way to the screams. Reggie felt that the entire store was rocking like a ship lost in a storm at sea. And then he heard the sound that was worse than yelling, worse than screaming, worse than knocking and worse than banging. He heard the sound of the end:

ding, ding, ding, ding, ding, ding, ding, ding, ding...

Blind

Malik Salaam

I have been blind for the majority of my natural life. When I say blind, I am speaking directly to the physical aspect of pupils and retinas. I am referring to the ability to look at concrete objects, and absorb height and width, color and texture, movement and light. You see... it's the very act of opening your eyelids so you can, oftentimes, carelessly scan the world.... A ceremony, which takes man/woman/child out of The Valley of Darkness and into.... Well, in all honesty, most of us never leave that valley mainly because our vision never extends beyond the surface.

*   *   *

Martin Luther King Jr. Drive, there is one in every city. And if my suspicion serves me correctly (suspicion being a lot more solid than assumption), then I'm willing to bet that Dr. King's namesake runs through impoverished neighborhoods all across this great nation. A man that dreamed of a day when people of different colors would sit at the same dinner table was not only gunned down like the main course, but to add insult to injury, his legacy has become the dark corners where crack kills. His dream has been reduced to the daily struggle of survival... schemes and scams... *What's your fuckin' angle, pimpin'? Nigga, get your hands out of my pocket!!!!*

I'm sorry.... Give me a second — sometimes the gift of being forced to view the world through the eyes of my soul, can be a curse, often sending me into a passionate whirlwind. The fact of the matter is that I have never traveled too far outside of Atlanta's city limits, and I have never been across the borders of Georgia – not physically. It has been so long since I was able to feel my pupils dilate. My vision is more like imagination.

The reality is, in all actuality, there are so many people in the world, all of them supposedly possessing their own points of view (whether original or attached to the chains of the flock), but reality is relative; therefore, it only exists in our individual imaginations. I mean, I ain't no James Baldwin, but I think the statement speaks volumes as to what life is about... or, should I say, our perception of what we imagine life is all about. Because we are all simply imagining.

My imagination is formed on sights unseen. I view my environment through which I can hear, smell, and touch. I visualize creation through the energy it exudes. I see the jam packed intersection of MLK and Ashby Street, with its horns screaming in frustration, engines roaring, and mufflers sending out warning shots. My imagination sketches in charcoal The Rib Shack with its bellows of gray smoke from slabs of flesh and bones as they slam against flaming hot metal grates. The sizzling sounds of fat. I smell home grown marijuana, mixed with the stench of cigarettes and liquor, as I maneuver around bodies that walk like they are alive, but send out no pulse from their souls.

I listen to them dying at night when glass is shattered and pistols settle the situation. My imagination takes snapshots of the captured splicing them with captions that read: Rico Shed Blood Over Bullshit. I see them dying, and it causes my soul disharmony. And even when I try to shut them out, in an attempt to find solace, my soul is shaken by their screams and pleas. Those voices that go unheard... those spirits that go unseen because they are hidden behind thumpin' bass lines and materials gained through the lives of the slain. That is until–the night the lights went out in Georgia.

I don't really consider myself totally aware of numerical time. For me, time is identified by movement, temperature, sounds, and moods. Morning in the inner-city is silent, and the night is overcrowded with the vibration of sound. Morning is filled with the quiet whispers of sorrow because today may very well be the same as yesterday. And night hums the singing of hymns and spirituals that beg not to face tomorrow.

*　　　　　　　*　　　　　　　*

Rico was always the rooster... it would usually happen somewhere after the congestion of rush hour... when the working class is left just that much more bewildered. Who knows the precise moment when Ricardo James peeled open his eyelids to stare at the surface? Who knows what were his first thoughts or if he had any. But what is known is that it was always his voice echoing in the dusk. The rattling of trunks. Tires locked, stocked and sliding across the over-worn asphalt. Cell phones. Buses. Children. The sounds of movement – all the soundtrack for a young man misled......

"Shit, shawdy, I 'ont even know..... But, please believe, it ain't like that in fuckin' Buckhead or fuckin' Vinnins.... Somewhere."

Unless he was on his cell phone, and even then he was never speaking directly to one individual. The sidewalk was Rico's stage, and his audience copped squats on front stoops.

"I bet you them muthafuckas power don't be off."

Rico's phone had an amplifier on its ringer. More than likely it was to notify the world that Rico was a hustler.

"*Riiiico.... Ain't shit, what's the bi'ness.... Naw, Black... Shit it's out over here.... Maaaan, I 'ont even know...Sound like that nigga Al...Shiiiitttt, I'm tryin to tell you, shawdy...Ya boy...Al-Qaida....Nigga, what...'Ey niggas better buckle up cause the night might get nasty... Boy....*

You see, inner cities create a need for survival and not in the natural, organic way. But a survival that blatantly defies every natural aspect of human existence. There may or may not be any official documentation of when the Black community adopted the whole "The world revolves around me, I don't give a Lincoln Continental about you, and I'll kill you before I see you live free" syndrome. One could easily argue that it has always been their reality.

Rico was a host for this syndrome. You could hear it in his language. There is, in the human voice, a tone that resounds past the surface level. It holds passion, pain, and happiness. The tone of one's voice can soothe or evoke terror simply by the tremble in the vocal cords. For Rico and his close knit Taliban of friends and/or foes, the tone simply translates to the success of survival is measured by the bottom line. Every action taken, every conversation, which erupted into fatality, the cars they bought, the females they mishandled, even the vicious pit bulls they trained to fight, all boiled down to a money green reduction. The loss of electricity that suddenly occurred throughout the State of Georgia, in Rico's imagination, was not a time for reflection or to come together with your loved ones. The Blackout meant simply that someone somewhere was not on their A-game, which made them a victim, and for Rico, that added up to dollar signs.

"Shit, that ol' man got so much money in there. He got to. He ain't got no job and he always be clean and shit. I bet he got about ten grand in there stuffed under his pillow. And he REALLY cain't see with these lights out."

The Old Man did have a substantial amount of money - this was true. But he wasn't simple minded enough to live on MLK his entire life and keep his money stashed under his pillow. And furthermore, it was also ridiculous to classify ten thousand dollars as "so much money." For Rico, though, it was enough to intrude on the old man's personal space.

All of the windows, which could be reached from ground level of the old man's estate, were barred, as was the front and back doors. So, Rico's only source of entry was through the crawl space connected to the basement that housed the hot water heater, like many old homes. As Rico used the strength in his forearms to snap the padlock, which secured the crawl space door, the excitement of his quickly approaching fortune made him snicker aloud. Maybe it wasn't just the money.

Maybe it was the ease in which he snapped the lock. Maybe it was his ability to see an opportunity in every situation, no matter how tragic, no matter how minuscule.

Whatever the thought that triggered the snicker, it was enough to send out an abrupt alert throughout the walls of the fortress. Something was happening out of the ordinary. The Old Man stopped caressing the pages of his book and opened the treasure chest drawer, which kept his birth certificate, social security card, and his semi-automatic .45 caliber pistol, easily accessible at all times. He listened carefully as the basement door was violently pried open. The sounds of unfamiliar feet fumbling in the dark…. The squeaking of steps…. The feeling of eminent danger sent the Old Man to crouch into what he considered to be the safest and darkest corner in his bedroom. The Old Man's index finger gently stroked the pistols trigger as his thumb flicked the safety to off.

He listened intently as doors were opened and closed and the contents of drawers were dumped onto his hardwood floors. The Old Man did not have a clue what evil spirit was floating through his safe space. But whoever it was must have considered themselves invisible due to the lack of electricity plaguing the neighborhood.

Rico was getting more and more frustrated as he rummaged through the Old Man's belongings. *Where the fuck does this ol' moafucka keep his bread?* His frustration was beginning to stir up his feelings of survival and violence. No longer was he slowly and quietly opening and closing cabinets and drawers. He was slamming and slinging things into the darkness. Rico ran up the stairs, two steps at a time, his flashlight bouncing its beams of the walls in the corridor, which lead to the Old Man's bedroom.

The Old Man's muscles tensed as he heard the door to his bedroom fly open. He could not physically see the individual that had so blatantly invaded his space. But he could hear him breathing. He could sense his anger and hate and greed. He could feel the warmth from his flashlight. He knew that whatever this evil spirit was meant him harm, and that his only way to survive was to bring this situation to a close.

Rico's face came to life, with an evil grimace, as he realized he was in the Old Man's bedroom. Rico could hear his own voice echoing in his head, *I bet he got about ten grand in there stuffed under his pillow.* Quickly, Rico flashed his light around the room until it landed on the king size bed. *Shiiiittt, it might be more than ten grand in this big moafucka.* In his excitement, Rico began to throw the pillows off of the bed, yanking the comforter, and almost in a fit of rage, he flipped the mattress. *Where the hell is this shit at?*

Nobody knows why it seemed as if somewhere in Rico's premature mind he blocked out the fact that he was, indeed, inside of the Old Man's house. Had he forgotten? Have we been so tricked that we can only see what we desire on the surface? When Rico reached for his hip, it was very evident that it dawned on him.

"Is that your ol' ass over there? Where the fuck do you keep the money at nigga?

The Old Man's breathing had increased. Fear creates a deafening sound, even in its silence. He knew the evil spirit heard it even before Rico's words were spoken. And then — a glow of light that warmed his face. It was the cock of a pistol. It was....danger.

*   *   *

I have been blind the majority of my natural life, that is, if you classify sight simply through the channels of one's pupils and retinas. You must understand that the reality is most people with 20/20 vision are actually blinder than I ever been or will ever be. For me, a tree is not simply wood and leaves. It is a fortress of peace and protection. It proclaims consistency and hope. Water is more than water. We, as a society, forget that it possesses the power of cleansing, the purity of spirituality.

I have been blessed to be able to view life. To be able to take in its colors through sounds and textures and energy, which it sends to my soul light years before its physical appearance is sketched in my imagination. Long before I splice them with captions that read: Rico was gunned down after breaking into a blind man's home, on Martin Luther King Jr. Drive, the night the lights went out in Georgia.

The Witnesses
by Amir Sulaiman

my heart won't think
but my mind refuses to feel
so it leaves me senseless
sleepless
restless
wandering
wondering
I only come to my senses
between sentences
and the sentence ends
without a period point
or without a point period
my points seem hollow
like hollow points
fired at point blank range
that would crack my brain
like my brain on crack
I'm between insane and black
stressed and brown
I'm a milky mulatto
passing
in the city of the living
passing and pretending as if I haven't died already
and I say I'm all ready
to do it again
because I'm a man of my word
and a man of my worth
and a man of the earth
I come from her and I'll return to the dirt
commune with worms
just can't let it take a turn for the worse
by passing and pretending
until I really believe that I'm living
and haven't died already
because I'm a man of the earth
and she will find me
and pull me to her bosom
until I can neither breathe nor speak
see nor blink

dream nor think
I think I'm dreaming
of a vanilla sky
and a chocolate earth
a caramel girl
that sings when she speaks
with perfume in her walk
her body transparent by how sincerely we talk
we'll take long walks
in gardens with rivers flowing beneath
what was old and grieved
is new and sweet
like sweet sweat
we're swept off of our feet
like souls solaced
in the sanctuary of God

in the precious presence of unspeakable beauty
the precious presence
is present, past and future
it is past time past space
time past away
never to come again
thy kingdom come
thy will be done
on earth as it is in heaven
and on earth I am missing heaven
so on earth I fear not my end I fear not of men
so on earth I fight demon and despot
the avaricious and the treacherous
with mercy in my fearlessness
and fire in my justice
love for the virtuous
and hatred for cowardice
why be a coward
how else do men ascend to their Lord
except by flying upon the wings of the Angel of Death

I'm a man of the earth
may she find me
and pull me to her bosom
until I neither breathe nor speak
see or blink
dream or think
I think I'm dreaming

of a vanilla sky
and a chocolate earth
a caramel girl
that sings when she speaks
with perfume in her walk
her body transparent by how sincerely we talk
we'll take long walks
in gardens with rivers flowing beneath
what was old and grieved
is new and sweet
like sweet sweat
we're swept off of our feet
like souls solaced
in the sanctuary of God

Crossing

Amir Sulaiman

I felt my soul leaving the place of dreams and entering the world of the mundane pain of reality. I whisper to myself, "There is no god but the one God."

I think I woke up at about 6:30 am. I didn't open my eyes until 7:05 a.m. I then, kept my eyes closed in the hollow hope that today was not today. I would be satisfied if today was tomorrow or even if today was yesterday. But it's not. Today is today. Today sits in my stomach, heavy like the Chinese food from my late and lonely yesterday night. I can already feel today taking its familiar seat at the base of my brain, applying an insurmountable pressure. I despise today for one reason only - today, I have to work.

I turn over on my right side to look out of my sixth story window. I stare down at the city streets, now swelling with busy worker ants in search of a cookie crumb that dropped to the concrete. This single crumb would be brought back home to feed more mouths than it could. Some of these people, I don't think, have the ambitious capacity to imagine having a whole cookie to themselves. I don't mean imagine in a fantasy sort of way, but rather, formulate an actual strategy. They probably couldn't even create that picture form in their minds. So they proceed to scavenge, like their mothers and fathers, for the American dream, crumb by crumb.

Now, growing frustrated by my fear of today, I rise defiantly to wash and dress. After my shower, I look in my closet to find only empty hangers swinging back and forth, as if to celebrate their freedom from the burden of my clothes. Quickly scanning the room, I find a pair of slightly wrinkled khaki pants that I hoped wouldn't be wrinkled after a couple hours of wear. I throw on a black long sleeve shirt that reads "Street Fatigues", in cream across the front. Walking into my boots, I proceed to the door and stumble down the stairs of my building.

Leaving my building, I am greeted by a vibrant sun and a gentle breeze. For a moment, I'm motionless to absorb life. The sunlight spills on the pair of tall oak trees and drips from their branches to make a beautiful intricate design on the concrete. A squirrel, which has learned not to trust me, runs up the oak and disappears in its bark. I decide I will embrace this day even if it does not desire my company or devotion.

My foot moves to take its first step onto the city sidewalk. This is one step into the urban maze of expected surprises that we call home. Some of us manage to stay sane. Most of us, however, fall into a kind of common insanity. Community craziness. Our abandonment of sanity is one of the only freedoms that we have cooperated in and have been successful in achieving.

The sidewalk grit grips my soles to hold me back or hold me down, but it does neither successfully. The tall buildings that surround me make me feel insignificant and trapped and protected. My concrete womb holds me tightly and I hope it will never let go. But I know it will, eventually, push me out into some other colder and larger world of trials and strangers. There is no doubt that the urban breath is an intoxicant. I feel invincible, which is a feeling that usually ends in death and/ or defeat.

At the intersection, I stop and look across the street to see the electric traffic sign that tells pedestrians when to walk and when it is not safe. A red hand, with its fingers together and palm facing us, shines out of the deep darkness of the metal yellow casing. Two pedestrians, a businessman - who is obviously busier than all of us - and I wait until this contraption, now letting off a rhythmic buzz, reassures us that the street is safe to cross. Its reassurance of safety is, appropriately, a white light in the form of a man in mid-stride.

Beside me, stands the businessman - the busy businessman. His white knuckles are gripping his attaché case. His index finger keeps tapping the leather, as if to keep time. Every second. *Tic, tap, tic, tap, tic, tap, tic, tap.* Every second. His head leans forward and his toes break the threshold of the curb. He's positioned to spit out of his blocks, as soon as the gun goes off. Why be in such a rush to a place you really don't want to be anyway? Anxiety moistens his temples. His collar is white clean and razor sharp. His silk tie wears more like a wooden cross hanging, pointing at his crotch. It is a sign of his initiation into the illustrious monetary monastery. He is not even one of the high priests, I don't think, but just a navy blue flunkey, wandering the back alleys of Wall Street. He can be found mumbling to himself, counting his dollars on his rosary beads. His cornflower blue noose is tight around his throat but hangs heavy without a branch to finish the job. I wonder if he sees the irony in pursuing freedom in stocks and bonds?

Unfortunately, he's a mediocre greyhound chasing the rabbit. I wish the dog knew that's not a real rabbit. I wish he knew that's not a real life. Only if he knew he is probably sprinting towards a divorce. Rushing towards custody suits that he won't win and promotions he won't get. He is chasing an ulcer and an early stroke. I hold my mouth and turn away. I would cry if it weren't so funny and I'd laugh if it weren't so sad.

An old woman, who also accompanies the busy businessman and me at the cross walk, flirts with a height of 5' 1". Her hair is brilliant in its whiteness, not a strand of brown, black or even gray. It makes circles and loops over her eyebrows and hides the most delicate part of her ears. She also stares up at the sign for affirmation. Her brown, fading eyes shoot up to push up her thin eyebrows and expose the bottom of her eyes. The whiteness of her eyes lacks the brilliance of her hair because of the tiny broken blood vessels. Her purse, which is held tightly to her body, appears to be heavier than she. I can't imagine what type of unnecessary things old women carry in those huge purses. I quickly renege on that thought because I have to admit that my grandmother has saved me on many occasions with the contents of her purse. I can remember gum, lotion, Vaseline, brushes, tissue (a whole box), matches, coupons, combs, potato chips, books, aspirin, tooth picks, cough syrup, Q-tips, deodorant, and even a 3 ½ inch computer disk, which I still haven't figured out because she didn't even have a computer then. She decided to wait until after the Y2K scare to buy hers.

Without warning, this woman suddenly stares up at me with a wide-eyed look of panic and desperation. Everything slows down, as my brain tries to understand. Her head violently starts to shake from left to right; but her eyes never blink or leave my eyes, and all the wrinkles around her mouth cooperate in making an oval. Out of this oval, in her face, blares a loud sound that I want to run and hide from. Her eyes bulge out like the eyes of a choking fish and begin to tear with terror. Her face of animal fright sends a shot of hot and stinging electricity up my spine and then to my head and face, which becomes warm with blood right under the skin's surface. Her expression is that of pleading, as if to ask me to help her. Actually, that is the scariest part of the whole thing because I don't know how to help her? Her short arm shoots out like an arrow and her short index finger points to the street.

I'm sure my eyes are moving like lightning towards the street; however; it feels like an eternity. The first thing my eyes notice is a brown leather attaché case suspended in mid-air, three feet above the ground. The rest of my observations happen simultaneously. I hear something that sounds like a frightened (or angry), wild elephant screeching at the top of his lungs. I soon realize that it is the sound of hot rubber on pavement, trying to stop two thousand pounds of moving steel. The sound raises a couple notes, with each fraction of a second, until it disappears into the high pitches above the human ear. That sound is the powerful, blunted thud that jars my body by just hearing it. My eyes capture the businessman as he sprawls on the hood of the car in a demented and silly fashion, his joints popping and limbs bending in inappropriate ways. He shoots his forehead through the windshield, as if to kiss the driver on the lips. His neck folds and creases, as his mouth could not make it all the way through the shattering glass.

The driver violently turns his four-door sedan - at about 40 mph to the right - in a futile attempt at dodging. He spins his car to face the direction he came from. This delayed effort pulls the rag doll, dressed in a three-piece suit, around the car to the driver side door. But before he is fortunate enough to finally hit the ground, the pole, holding the white light of the man in mid-stride, interrupts his descension. His upper torso is trying to defend the pole from the car door or the car door from the pole, but to no avail. The car meets the pole and embraces it in a perverted gesture of affection. Then everything is still.

Four or five screams, that I don't really hear, ring out in the distance. I wish I could express what they did, but I can't. I feel a sharp numbness that starts in my chest and spreads throughout my soul's system, causing me to forget to breath. When I remember, I can't. My legs threaten that they will soon disobey my order to hold up the rest of my body. A strange cold sweat rises from the pores under my "Street Fatigue" shirt. Wetness is also gathering in my boxer shorts, which I hope are that same cold sweat. The heavy Chinese in my stomach seems not as heavy anymore. Rather, it is more like thick and wet helium rising to my throat. Without my permission, my body forcefully yanks my chest over my waist and jerks my jaws open, causing my eyes to water. Fortunately, no noodles, but instead, a powerful heave and a heavy saliva spills from my bottom lip, as my stomach violently pumps and twits.

My eyes find the driver. He is also donning the robes of the monetary monastery. His religious scripture must have spilled from his attaché case and whirls like a paper tornado in the interior of his sedan. A thin flowing layer of perspiration covers his face and seeps to soil his white, clean collar. His head moves slowly and gently back and forth. His mouth holds a shape that resembles a smile, but its awkward twist exposes his trauma. His eyes move quickly and everywhere and yet, are unable to focus on anything. Finally, his eyes find his collarbone peeking at him through the broken skin of his shoulder. The saturation of blood has given his cornflower blue cross a nice, deep purple color. His brow jumps and his eyes finally seek refuge behind their lids. His neck relaxes and he retreats into an infant sleep.

The old woman grabs my hand (not in a way to comfort me but to keep herself from falling). Her nails are short and dull; however, that does not stop her from breaking my skin - inflicting a pain I appreciate because it also breaks my numbness. Her other shaking wrinkled hand covers her mouth and her eyes finally overflow, not from sympathy, but still from shock. I want to hold her in my arms, but I change my mind.

Slowly my body, mind, and soul return to normal. My lungs fill with oxygen to make up for the lost breaths. My stomach stabilizes, and I thank God for stopping me from releasing my bladder until a more appropriate time. The woman lets go of my hand, only for it to accompany her other hand over her mouth. She continues to sob (now from sympathy) and call on God. I do not start to cry nor do I have the desire to. People begin to crowd around and I see the flashing light of police and ambulances. I refuse to be a part of the familiar street scene of vulgar, open-mouth amazement. The police start with their *"Go home, folks, there's nothin' to see here"* speech. I take the advice of the policeman, continuing down the street the way I was going, and secretly rejoicing in the chance I've been given to go to work.

Only when he has ceased to need things can a man truly be his own master and so really exists.

— Anwar Sadat, third president of Egypt.

www.goodestuffentertainment.com

www.goodestuffentertainment.com

Printed in the United States
27185LVS00001B/230

9 780971 209503